NO LONGER DENYING SEXUAL ABUSE

MAKING THE CHOICES THAT CAN CHANGE YOUR LIFE

KIM O'HARA

North Carolina

Published in the United States by WriteLife Publishing
(An imprint of Boutique of Quality Books Publishing Company, Inc.)
www.writelife.com

978-1-60808-279-7 (p)
978-1-60808-280-3 (e)

Library of Congress Control Number: 2022951885

Book design by Robin Krauss, www.bookformatters.com
Cover design by Rebecca Lown, www.rebeccalowndesign.com

First editor: Allison Itterly
Second editor: Andrea Vande Vorde

PRAISE FOR
NO LONGER DENYING SEXUAL ABUSE
AND AUTHOR KIM O'HARA

"This book is truly a gift to sexual abuse survivors. Kim O'Hara delivers a courageously candid and insightful depiction of her devastating experience as a survivor of incest. She recounts how the denial and shame associated with keeping this secret can lead to dysfunctional and chaotic behaviors. In her relatable and down-to-earth voice, Kim illustrates the healing power of therapy when you find the right therapist fit. She shows how the answer is not to suffer in silence but to process the trauma in a safe environment. Readers of *No Longer Denying Sexual Abuse: Making the Choices That Can Change Your Life* will feel like they are listening to the story of a good friend. They will find a kindred spirit in Kim O'Hara and know that they are not alone. This book will inspire readers to take steps to heal from their own trauma and regain control over their lives."

   – **Bonnie Zucker, PhD**, Clinical Psychologist in Los Angeles

---

"Profound, deeply authentic, and painfully honest, Kim O'Hara's message is a call to arms and the manual to bring victims of sexual abuse back to the truest essence of themselves. Beautifully written, Kim's story gives us insight into the devastation that young children endure as they silently deny the burden and deep shame of emotional and sexual abuse. Kim embraces her truth by stepping out of the shadows to understand for the first time a child's limited ability to understand this warped reality. Her sudden awakening in adulthood to finally see herself as whole gives victims both the validation and the courageous steps to recalibrate life and boldly take their power back. *No Longer Denying Sexual Abuse: Making the Choices That Can Change Your Life* is a must read and an invaluable message of hope and resilience."

– **Andrea Mein DeWitt,** Coach and Author of *Name, Claim & Reframe: Your Path to a Well-Lived Life*

"The world needs truthtellers—and this is precisely what Kim O'Hara has shown up to do. By facing her own truth of sexual abuse and sharing it in all its pain and messiness, she paves the way for other survivors to step forward from the shadows of their own. And when one survivor heals a part of themselves, we all do. It takes courage to tell the truth . . . and to heal. This is an invitation to do both."

– **Kristen Noel,** Editor-in-Chief *Best Self Magazine*

"Kim O'Hara has written a triumph. Her story held me spellbound as she revealed the answers to life challenges far beyond those stemming from sexual abuse. There is not one person who will not benefit and grow from the lessons learned through her journey. A must read for deep insights in self growth."

– **Naomi Joseph,** Author, *Binge and Sprint: From Endless Cake to Recovery*

TABLE OF CONTENTS

FOREWORD

I had been molested as a child and was told to keep quiet by the adults who should have protected me, and I never thought much about it again. The abuse only happened once, and I knew about other kids who had experienced violent or ongoing stories of molestation, so I shrugged it off as something I shouldn't make a big deal about and stuffed it away as a young child. As a struggling young adult, I made devastating choices that put me in the hands of unsafe sexual predators over and over again, and I could never figure out why I seemed to be such an easy target. Today, I am clean and sober. My last drink was because I "came to" in a jarring moment while having sex with someone (or was it rape?) who had restrained me without my consent and had possibly drugged me. Because of my autism, it's also possible that I was in major meltdown at that time and was unable to speak or advocate for myself. It was inexplicably traumatic, and I had no ability to process it all except to think, *If I wasn't drinking, none of this would have happened.* I stopped drinking from that day forth. A final act of self-protection after a demoralizing bottom of powerlessness in every sense of the word. I had struggled to protect myself for nearly my entire adult life up until that point, and I felt tremendous suicidal shame that I was to blame for the awful situations I put myself in while reliving those various forms of sexual abuse.

When I was five years into sobriety, a script arrived for me to play the mom of a young girl who had been molested by a family friend. After reading the script, my body convulsed for hours in dry-heaving vomits as I sobbed uncontrollably. I couldn't even finish my shift at the diner, and my boss saw the hysterical state I was in and sent me home with paternal care. This unexpected release from my body was triggered because I was finally stable enough in my life to handle what had happened to me decades ago. All this time, it was hiding beneath the surface, subconsciously driving my self-destructive, sabotaging behaviors, and I had no idea of it. I played it off, just like Kim talks about in this book, when any mention of sexual abuse came up (as if what happened to me wasn't that big of a deal because it only happened once in my memory.) So I started writing about my experience, just to unpack it all. I realized I was the one carrying the burden of shame from that event, as if I had done something bad. I remembered my abuse: I was seven years old, and a forty-something-year-old man had touched me inappropriately. A close family member had asked me out of the blue one day if I'd ever been inappropriately touched by this man. My family member had guessed my secret but told me that I needed to stay quiet about what had happened, forever. So, as a young child, I did what I was told. The secret ate at me for decades and made it nearly impossible to have intimate relationships. Now as an adult, I couldn't be silent anymore.

By the grace of a power greater than myself, a fellow recovery member who was well into his healing journey from childhood sexual abuse, and then violent jail rape, saw an article I'd posted about my molestation and put me in touch with Kim. I had read an earlier draft of her book and cried my way through it, resonating with how authentic and honest she was about her own experience, strength, and hope through incest, and how imperfect life was because of it. I knew what she was talking about and finally felt safe disclosing my own experiences to her as a fellow survivor who is striving toward wholeness. I wrote two drafts of my own memoir because of her vulnerability and transparency.

It was life changing because it allowed me the freedom to give a voice to the little girl who had been silenced about the abuse I had suffered in more ways than one, which led me to be suicidal when I was fifteen years old.

Read this book if it's in your hands. Give it to your friends if you know it's what they need. Trust yourself again. Find your place in the world. Know that you are not irreversibly damaged. You will find a tribe that gets it. Love each other. Play again. And know that you deserve success above and beyond your wildest dreams because what happened to you does not get to decide who you are. This is what I found on my journey with Kim and her words. May you find the same.

Sue Ann Pien, actress, director, and space enthusiast

INTRODUCTION

To publish this book, I had to trust in the depths of my sexual abuse recovery to see how brightly I could shine in order for others to blossom as I had. Another part of me still wanted to bury the truth, which is understandable given that I am a different person now than the person I was in my past. I am nine years into recovery from sexual abuse, eight years without having a drink or a drug, and seven years running my own business. As I was writing this book, I thought, *Do I really want to share the troubling and erratic behaviors that defined who I was in my sexual abuse denial?* The answer is clearly yes. You would not be reading this book about my tumultuous denial and raw recovery if you weren't looking to heal.

While I wish I had never been abused, it is where I began. And now you can begin again. I am here for you. If you are coming to terms with sexual abuse or haven't yet properly mourned a long-lost life, you have found a home here. *No Longer Denying Sexual Abuse* is a guide for any abuse survivor, no matter what stage of recovery you are in. This book is not intended to replace twelve-step programs or therapy. It is a strong companion to navigate the trickery and deception of suppressed abuse memories, as well as mourning the carnage along the way. It's time to examine your shame and self-loathing and rise like a phoenix from the ashes to become a greater version of yourself. It's about the lie that the abuse didn't happen, a lie that disguised itself in what it could find to be a distraction—addiction, self-abandonment, isolation, depression, and low self-worth. It's about being unable to be intimate with yourself and others under the shroud of anger and isolation. I had suppressed the truth that I was a sexual abuse survivor to the point where I knew I was surviving but did not know from what. Every day, I waged wars with the unknown inside and outside of myself. Then one day I woke up and knew. I wasn't taking back the happiness; I was creating it for the first time. I was equally excited and terrified.

I am not "fixed," but I am not broken either. Today I am fully whole. I am proud of the woman I am and the decisions I make on a daily basis about how to treat myself and others. There are still parts of me that were created as a result of the conditioning of my childhood abuse that may never go away. For example, trust issues. If I am in a new relationship with someone I don't know well enough, I look for the signs that I am being deceived. This is referred to as "stinking thinking" in Alcoholics Anonymous (AA), and it is exacerbated by the abuse. When I tell my therapist about it, she says with a steady gaze, "Did you think with your upbringing you would easily just trust?" In theory, I know how tremendously blessed my life is, but at the same time, I am still working on looking over my shoulder for when the tragedy will strike.

The power I've discovered in my healing has saved me in this jagged and sweet journey to recover from abuse and its denial. I've never stopped searching and seeking. The anger has dissipated from a furious rage to a mild irritation. Now I can look at myself objectively and say, "Girl, you are spinning out. Focus on the good. Get back to seeking." I no longer see self-preservation as an antidote to intimacy. I am not damaged goods. I am deserving of love.

The voice inside me loved to criticize and beat me up with old stories. *You always make it to the one-yard line but never score a touchdown. You are a starter but not a finisher.* I would tell the voices to shut up because I just couldn't bear the possibility that they were right. I had to live, and even if I didn't want to dredge up the past, I had to embrace the whole me—all the parts, even the ones that felt dirty and shameful. I have learned that if you want to do something right, you have to put your whole heart into it, or just wait. I couldn't wait any longer. I needed to get this book out of me and into the world. I needed you to read it so you could stop criticizing and demoralizing yourself. A group hug won't fix the long-term effects of denial, but seeing how it has affected every nook and cranny of your life will gradually help you realize that waiting to heal is no longer an option.

Through the evolution of this book and my recovery from sexual abuse, I navigated romantic relationships (broke a few hearts, had my heart broken), grew my book coaching business, launched a podcast, bought a house, continued my sobriety, and reshaped who I was as a mother and friend. I saw the benefits of what writing the book had done for me. I face the world differently now that I understand the balance of conflict and love. While I was still anxious, scared, and hesitant, I was also leaning into the manifestation of bigger dreams and speaking my truth. I was fearlessly learning to trust in my patience, which came from a quiet confidence in my intuition.

Recovery from sexual abuse is no joke. I am still stunned when I read my words about how difficult it was to endure. The terror, the pain, the fear, and the barely hanging on. Yet, I made the choice to walk through it, and I know you can too. Today I no longer live in my trauma, but I also understand its power. I respect the facts, but I don't let them control my life. Trust me, I am walking through some fires right now in my life, but not in the same way. My hope is that when you read my story, you will realize that you are not alone, that you can be better, and one day you will be there for other survivors as an example of how good life can be.

When you make choices to change your life, you commit to getting better and being honest about how abuse has affected you, but don't let it prevent you from becoming the person you are meant to be. You will be astounded by what you are capable of creating when you have discernment and agency over your decisions. You will have the courage, strength, and a voice to continue healing, growing, and discovering a new you on a whole new level. You will be able to look back on everything you did in the past in abuse denial and choose to forgive yourself. You will understand the changes that need to be made at a cellular level. You can heal the abuse from your DNA so you don't pass it on to your children. I hope that by reading my stories, you will be able to reflect on your own story and ascend to the throne of life that awaits you.

I had repressed my abuse in my subconscious mind for over four decades and didn't remember it until I had a dream. Just one dream, one night, and everything became clear to me. I could have stuffed that moment back inside and said, *hell no*. But the time had come to know more, to be more. To be free of the stench and soil of the repression. When you decide it is time to face sexual abuse, you have to fight and claw and scratch for early understanding. "Why? Why?" I yelled into tunnels, only to hear my own voice yelling back. I didn't know who would ever hear me because I had lost all faith in therapists who failed to detect the abuse, husbands who didn't see I was hurting inside, and parents who denied the abuse. Today, I listen to all the messengers who come to me. I believe in the angels that want me to see and hear, even if it means walking away from people who don't serve my highest good. I deserve deep self-love, and so do you.

I am releasing this book to proudly stand tall as the woman I have become by sharing the woman I used to be. I may no longer be her, but I once was her, and I can stand in your shoes and tell you to walk with me.

Do not regret the past as you walk a new path.

One day, the sun will shine down on your face while you're enjoying a lovely day in the park. You will be with your children or your pet, and you'll feel the warmth for the first time in a way you've never felt it before. You'll hear a loud laugh, look around, and realize that the laughter came from you. You'll discover that you like wearing blue blazers and taking twenty-minute naps in the middle of a workday because you damn well deserve it. You'll learn how to be the best version of yourself for all the wonderful people in your life. Does that sound like a fairy tale? Far from it.

Every chapter in this book focuses on a specific topic of recovery and healing. I share my personal stories in each chapter, and I do not shy away from the brutal honesty of my experiences with rage, addiction, sexuality, and a disconnect from my inner self or any form of spirituality. In the process of choosing a better life, you will gain insight into the person you are slowly rediscovering you were born to be.

The chapters in this book unravel all the conditioning that developed from the secret repression of sexual abuse. Part of this process is having the choice to tell others: significant others, spouses, parents, children, and friends. You were abused, and you have been hurt. The more I healed my soul, the more God pointed me toward the people I love. I either told them about the abuse or behaved in a manner that reflected my healing. As you embark on your recovery journey, people you love will notice you changing. How could they not when you are radiating your unique original self for the first time?

We also have bodies that need to be reclaimed. They were used for another person's pleasure, desire, or anger. One time is all it takes for damage to occur. We get to take our bodies back. I was a sex and love addict for a very long time. I had a low opinion of my body. I rarely ever thought of it as a temple unless I felt I looked hot or fit. That opinion manifested into attracting romantic partners who didn't truly align with my values. You deserve to be in a healthy, romantic relationship.

You will also find your inner child—the young version of yourself who screams for attention and healing. I was resistant to my inner child, but writing allowed me to become the adult who could parent her and let her be a child again. It was key to my newfound happiness.

The old and abused you will die on this journey so the new and beautiful you can shine.

The topics discussed in this book reveal how my life gradually changed as I peeled back the old skin of a silent sexual abuse victim. The act of getting sober from drugs, alcohol, and sex addiction, as well as finding meditation, spirituality, and a god of my understanding were a reflection of that change. My relationship with God was crucial in my recovery, but this will look different for everyone. Whether or not you believe in God, having a strong spiritual foundation will help guide you to be the best version of yourself.

One of my goals in writing this book is for you to discover how strong you really are and to unearth the courage it takes to step out of your pain and do something you never thought possible. When you are on the path to healing, you will make stronger commitments and put yourself first. You will live in the integrity of the person you were born to be before your identity was scarred by the abuse. After hiding in the shadows, I realized I desired a greater visibility, and I hope we can stand in the spotlight together.

In each chapter, I offer exploratory exercises and guidance on how to heal from the denial of sexual abuse. There are thought-provoking questions at the end of each chapter that serve as a foundation for further healing. While keeping a journal is not required, I strongly encourage you to have one in order to complete all of the exercises, which may include more extensive writing.

This journey can be both illuminating and confusing, so I offer insights on how to take a moment to pause and avoid overload. Recovery doesn't have a finish line. We each have our own timeline for our soul healing, so I can't tell you when you'll be done. All I can say is to keep working and to celebrate the changes you see in yourself. Take note of the good things that start to come into your life. Unfold at your pace. This work is delicate, but there is a warrior waiting to be discovered.

I am a survivor of incestuous sexual abuse, but I am not a victim. I am resilient and mentally healed, allowing me to participate in life on a more soulful and grateful level. I want all of this for you. As you read this book, you will slough away the painful dirty layers of yourself to expose the shining bright light within. You will gain permission to accomplish great things, and you will receive new tools to thrive.

My hope in writing this book is to help one person at a time be lifted from the shameful secret of sexual abuse. Then that one survivor will call out to another, and another, and another. When you have finished reading this book, pass it on to someone who is hurting so that they, too, can heal from their painful past. Through our powerful healing, we can collectively grow as women and men capable of changing the face of the world. We have a calling greater than what we could have imagined because we have survived. We are the kings and queens, the leaders, and the change agents of the world, and it is our responsibility to go out there and make that change happen.

Success, recovery, new perspectives, and enlightenment is not an overnight job. You have been in the darkness, but now you can join me in the light. Let's become incredible, vulnerable, honest, self-aware, and determined people. We will no longer hide behind the secret of sexual abuse denial.

Chapter 1
REMEMBERING

No survivor wants to remember the abuse for the first time. For many, the subconscious mind obstructs the memory until there is some kind of sign that your emotional maturity has evolved to handle the short-term or long-term decimating effects of realizing that sexual abuse is part of your story. You awaken to this truth, and you can't erase it. While you may not want to remember, there is the golden gate to the life on the other side that has been obstructed for so long. The person inside of you who could not seek the light—the divine you who was in the darkness for so long—gets to step out and begin a new chapter. No more limping along. No more dialing it in. You get to begin a new life that is firmly rooted in truth. Will you face all the facts the day after you remember? No. The week after? Perhaps not.

According to the International Society for Traumatic Stress Studies, it is common for people who experienced a traumatic event to remember the event after a long delay. "At the time of the traumatic event, the mind makes many associations with the feelings, sights, sounds, smells, taste, and touch connected with the trauma. Later, similar sensations may trigger a memory of the event."[1] So when you remember the abuse, it may seem like it comes out of nowhere. *Why now?* you may ask. It feels radically inconvenient, but honestly, there is no good time to recall abuse.

---

[1] "Recovered Memories of Childhood Trauma," International Society for Traumatic Stress Studies, accessed July 1, 2022, https://istss.org/public-resources/trauma-basics/what-is-childhood-trauma/remembering-childhood-trauma.

It took forty-two years for my mind and body to remember the sexual abuse because my subconscious had buried it so deep. It was a way for my mind to protect me from my trauma so I could be high functioning—gaining work accolades or building my family—under the shadow of a very big, dark secret that festered over time. Once I remembered the abuse, I didn't have the choice to ignore it. I had to face the abuse head-on.

When you face the abuse of denial, you will be combing through the details. For a while, you will be living in an uncomfortable space between the past you and the new you. In that chasm, you will see that there is a direct route and path to happiness, and the outcome is your new life. Your time for self-awareness has arrived. There is no ending to this journey, just a beginning.

REMEMBERING MY STORY

I will never forget the day when I first remembered I had been abused. It was December 2012, and I was forty-two years old. The heat of the afternoon sun blasted through the window as I sat in stunned silence in my living room. I had woken up from a dream that morning and was still in an altered state of the past. It was a dream like none I had ever had before. The visceral, slightly blurred visual, the heightened sound. The shallow crunch on the carpet of footsteps down the hall. The black shadow those feet made in the light under the door to my childhood bedroom. The doorknob turning. When that door opened and I saw my father standing there, I knew I had been abused by him. I had wanted to vomit in my dream, but I was also in the disassociated body of myself as a little girl. I was almost catatonic as I sat in my living-room chair, thinking, *How many times did he abuse me? Ten, twenty?* It was too soon to know, but the repetition didn't matter at that moment. The one-time recall was enough. I could still feel his breath on me from the dream. I couldn't yet access what it was like to be that little girl except for a pervading fear. I was a scared little girl. So scared I didn't tell anyone for forty-two years, including myself.

Now I am remembering.

It sucks.

I hate it.

For four decades, I had repressed the truth that I was a sexual abuse survivor. Somehow, I knew subconsciously that I was surviving, but I did not know from what. Every day of my life, I waged wars with the unknown both inside and outside of me.

Since facing my denial, I've witnessed women in AA meetings remember their abuse while also realizing that they were not at fault. The transition happens from believing they were a bad girl who invited the abuse to realizing they were objectified. Remembering the abuse can change over time as you heal other parts of yourself, such as getting sober or going to therapy. Your self-worth and self-love grow and change as you recall your past. Women have told me, "I thought I invited it," or, "If I told anyone, they would hurt my family." We can begin to heal when we speak out about what transpired and face the full extent of the memory.

After I came to terms that my abuse dream was in fact the truth, I tried to wrap my head around what had happened. Sadly, my first thought was not one of self-compassion. My first feelings were not of sadness or loss, nor of empathy for the young girl who'd lost her childhood. Instead, I wondered what other people would think of me and whether they would believe me. Then the self-doubt crept in. I wondered if I had been lying to myself about what had happened to me because I wanted attention. Then I chastised myself for even thinking such a thing. What kind of attention was I looking to attract? *Hey, everyone, I am a sexual abuse survivor of incest. Come be my friend!* I don't think so.

I had to think long and hard about who could handle this

icky truth. I wondered who I could confess to. Yes, *confess*, as if I were complicit to it, an active participant when I was four, six, or eight years old. But it still felt like a confession to me.

Then there was the question, almost an awe, of how long the abuse memories had been suppressed in my subconscious. My mind had tricked me! *My God, what else is not real?* I questioned. But my mind did not bury the truth because it hates me, but because it loves me and didn't think I could handle it. And I probably couldn't handle the truth until that day. On the surface, it may not have seemed like the perfect time for the abuse to reveal itself, but at that point in my life, I had grown up just enough. I had made demands on my spiritual life and my marital life, and I had started to take a hard look at my addictions. The dream appeared because I was ready. Was I like Buddha on the mountaintop? Hell no! In many ways, I was still as frozen as that eight-year-old girl in the dream, but my adult self was signaling to my inner child that I was ready.

THE AFTERMATH OF REMEMBERING

As you heal from your past, the negative voice in your head will tell you that you brought the abuse on. But this is far from the truth. That voice is the shamed and abused child within you who believes he or she did something wrong by participating. The voice is not the adult you who knows you did not comply, or if you did, you had no choice.

Your ego wants you to continue being the same person you have always been because that is how it knows you. "Stay safe, don't shine, and we will make it through," your ego says. If you want a bigger life and to pursue your dreams as a new authentic self, you have to break up with your ego for a while.

The timing of remembering is never perfect, and it is guaranteed to be messy. You will reflect on some very dark, manipulative behaviors and the parts of yourself that you have to discard officially. In order to do that, you still have to suffer through those behaviors to gain a better understanding of your modus operandi (denial for survival) before you can discard them. I was forty-two when my subconscious decided to reveal my abuse to me, and I believed its message. I could have pushed it back, but I knew I had no other choice. The time had come for me to move forward emotionally in a much bigger way.

After I came to the realization that I had been abused, shit hit the fan big time. I had spent a lifetime believing that I was in control of my life even though I had addictions—alcohol and sex—as well as tremendous amounts of rage and chaos. I had no idea I was hiding a secret; I just assumed I was misunderstood and edgy. I went through life feeling naturally tough. *Don't mess with me, people.* I had a false sense of security and bravado that told me I was unstoppable and could handle any confrontation. I didn't care whether or not someone liked me. I often thought people were out to get me or were going to mess with me in some way. When I suspected someone was deceiving me, my distorted trust erupted in rage. I went from docile to rageful in 2.3 seconds and blindsided people. It's a miracle I had as many girlfriends as I did, but I only kept two long-term friends because I moved around so much between states, colleges, or cities. They saw me at my worst, so I trusted them completely, and still do. In my recovery, I've realized that everyone has their own perspective, feelings, and issues, and rarely is it a diabolical plan to mess with me. They are just being human and dealing with their own shame or issues. I still feel it when my edges are bumped or a core wound is rubbed, but I don't act on it.

At the time of the dream, my second marriage had ended. My ex-husband had moved out, and I was a single parent of our two little girls in our once-shared apartment. He would visit the girls and take them out. It was a sad time for everyone because divorce can be like a death. I had a part-time job at Trader Joe's. Twelve-step recovery in AA and in Sex and Love Addicts Anonymous (SLAA) helped me to get clean on my addictions and have clarity. It was time for me to move on from my marriage and work on learning more about who I really was.

I rehashed the past after realizing the truth of my dream, scrambling to figure out why I didn't know about the abuse. In an aha moment, two instances stood out to me. I had been tipped off to the abuse twice in prior years.

The first time was when I was twenty-one years old and partying with my dad and one of his girlfriends, as well as my first husband, at my dad's country club. My dad was definitely an alcoholic, but the concept of AA was so foreign to me at the time that I identified him as my hard-partying forty-seven-year-old dad. Drinking with my dad, and the money he spent at the bar, felt like fraternal love.

At one point, I went to the bathroom and my dad's girlfriend followed me. We were both pretty wasted. Before she entered the stall, she leered at me and asked, "Did your dad ever sexually abuse you?"

The wind had been knocked out of me. It was such a bizarre question. I tried to think through the thick pall of alcohol, but I couldn't come up with a response. My ego said, *This lady is a nut bag, and I won't believe it.*

"Why did you ask me that?" I asked her as we washed our hands.

"Because he told me he did," she said, drunkenly smug, drying her hands.

I leaned against the cool tile wall of the bathroom, strained nonchalance. "That's ridiculous," I said.

She stared at me with apathy. "Really?" she said.

"Really!" I replied. "He's a drunk who's talking crap."

"Okay," she said. "It's your life." That was the end of it.

I felt sick to my stomach, so I stuffed it down. Erased it out. Denial and acknowledgment had been in the ring in a cage fight, and denial had won without any bloodshed. We went back to the bar and drank until the last call. I even drove my drunken dad and his girlfriend home, a foggy sense in my brain, like a surreal hell, as they laughed in the back seat.

Her words played over and over in my head: *Did he abuse you?*

I think I may have even put my dad to bed that night. Sloppy drunken idiot.

I buried that conversation down so damn deep. I made sure it would never resurface. I told no one. I don't remember telling my first husband, or if I did, I told him as if it were a joke and that woman was a crazy drunk. I locked that shit away for years. I never even thought about it again. Denial is such a powerful tool for survival. Denial wins if you are not ready. On that day, I wasn't ready to hear the message that I had been abused. Denial is profoundly deep even when there are tip-offs.

The second time I had an indication of the abuse was a sensation I felt entirely in my own body. It was 2006, and my daughter was ten months old at the time. I was in my thirties living with my first husband in San Jose, California. My dad had impulsively moved to California after spending his entire life in Rhode Island where we are originally from. He showed up with a sparse collection of belongings recklessly tossed into the back of a leased Grand Cherokee. I assumed he was there to clock in some grandpa time with his first granddaughter. Like any new mother who had limited help, I was eager to hand him the baby and run an errand.

While I was shopping at the mall, a panicked feeling overcame me. I would later learn in abuse recovery that this tool was a powerful intuition that I could use for good and to walk away from bad situations in life. But when I was in the mall, all I knew was that I needed to get home immediately because something was seriously wrong. I drove wildly and burst into the house to find my dad in my daughter's bedroom. He was playing airplane with one of her stuffed animals while she was on the changing table. I felt immediate relief, as if I had just saved my daughter from something, though I had no conscious idea what. I snatched her up and told him right then and there that he would never babysit her again.

My dad died a week later of a third heart attack on my sister's couch. I am confident that nothing happened to my daughter that day, but if he had not died, the abuse could have been passed down to the next generation. I could have had a change of heart and let him babysit. I may not have gotten that intuitive hit a second time.

I believe my father's death so soon after this incident was either God hearing my prayers and ending my father's life before he could do any more harm to the women in the family, or my father's soul could do no more damage and his own heart stopped beating. My dad died with both of our secrets, which made it difficult for me to dislodge them. Instead, I spent another eight years of substance abuse addiction, drinking alcohol, and smoking marijuana to numb my feelings. At that point, I had been steadily drinking and using drugs for most of my adult life. Despite feeling isolated and unhappy in a suburban neighborhood far from my creative outlets in Los Angeles, I planned to have a second baby.

Every year that passed, the repressed truth made my life a little uglier, a little messier, and a little more addictive. I carried a heavier and heavier burden every single day. I struggled with my marriage, career, addiction, motherhood, depression, migraines, and I could never settle into anywhere to live and feel happy. The secret of my sexual abuse ruled my actions and personality for four decades.

So, in comparison, the dream wasn't so bad.

STARTING THE PROCESS

The day after my abuse dream, I called the couples' therapist I had seen with my second husband, my children's father. She was a perfectly fine counselor, trying to mend a relationship that was long over. I didn't know where else to turn, and she had a way of talking to me in the sessions that suggested she had a deeper view of my anger.

"I was abused," I sobbed to her over the phone. "I need help. Can I come see you? Can you help me?"

After consoling me, she told me she had a wonderful referral. Then, and I can't explain why, I called my ex-husband. Maybe I was fueled by guilt or shame, but it felt important that he knew because he was the key person I had lived with during the previous decade of denial. It was my first tiny step toward recovery from the sheath of shame.

"I was abused," I said as tears streamed down my face.

"Oh," he responded. "That explains everything."

I didn't talk to him about it after that.

Recovering from sexual abuse is not an easy path, and it looks different for everyone. When we remember the abuse, we may not know who to tell right away. There are so many layers to uncover in order to let go and heal. It took me nine years to get where I am today—and that was a combination of everything in this book, including therapy, spiritual retreats, AA meetings, and a variety of uncomfortable and joyous scenarios that I had explored in my new self-awareness. Regardless of the modalities, actions, or time, what is most important to understand is that you now have a choice to get better and heal. Your choices were taken away when you were sexually abused, but now is the time to take back your power.

The process of beginning to heal from denial and empowering yourself is rooted in a steadiness. You want to be gentle with how fast you move to unpeel the onion. You don't want to re-traumatize yourself in the race to get better. I have only benefited from allowing time and space to heal me. When I rushed in recovery, whether it was being a personal development junkie or not deregulating when I felt emotionally overwhelmed, it didn't harm me, but I felt depleted. You don't have to rush out and tell everyone you know about the abuse. You can start by wrapping your arms around yourself and loving yourself.

Here are a few things to consider after you remember the abuse:

Sit in the simple awareness that the abuse happened

Taking on a new role as an abuse survivor can be a transition, and you may play with different identities in your head. You could call yourself a "trauma thriver," or maybe you don't consider yourself a survivor at all. Understand that as you give your situation a voice, your awareness will change and continue for years. For now, just sit in the new awareness without an agenda.

Share your story with other survivors

Listen when someone talks about their own abuse. See what they share and then ask if you can share your story with them. These people don't even have to be the best of friends. You are practicing saying out loud, "I am a survivor of sexual abuse." One of the most emotional moments for people who come to AA is the first time they say out loud, "My name is X, and I am an alcoholic." This context is the same. There are several support groups, such as SLAA and group therapy for survivors, that can help with such a personal revelation.

Be prepared to have moments of extreme anger and sadness

You can go from being really pissed off and wanting to retaliate to feeling remorse about lost time. I can assure you that these mood swings from anger to sadness will pass, but for right now, it is important to feel your emotions.

Find solace in prayer

Even if you are not a religious person, find a way to pray. Whether it is saying affirmations like "I love myself" in the mirror or sitting in the sand at the ocean and marveling in the abundance of nature. Prayer is a connection to your most loving self. Pray for the willingness to move past the pain of remembering so you can start to live the life of your wildest dreams.

Today, I get to tell my story to anyone who is in denial and encourage them to face the truth when it appears. And if you're like me and it doesn't happen until there's a lot of wreckage, that is perfectly okay too. You are going to get better now and make up for all the damage by loving yourself fully, soothing your inner child, and coming to terms with your adult state.

It's time to start living your real life and finally heal.

THOUGHT-PROVOKING QUESTIONS

Have you told anyone about your realization that you were abused? What is holding you back?

Can you believe that remembering will offer you a life of freedom?

It is often an outsider who tips you off to the possibility of abuse. Did someone in your past suggest to you that you were abused? Forgive yourself if you didn't acknowledge it at the time. We are ready to deal with it when we are able and not a minute sooner.

Chapter 2
UNDERSTANDING YOUR PAST

As a survivor of abuse and denial, I meet men and women who exhibit behaviors that lead me to believe they have been abused. I meet them often in my recovery circles, as they try to unearth their truth that lies behind the grip of addiction. In most cases, I find that a part of you freezes at the age when you were abused, and this follows you into adulthood until you come to terms with your past and recreate a new present. So many of us feel like children when we tell our stories. It can be confusing when we have adult jobs, responsibilities, and children of our own.

No matter what your story or situation is, we all share the same sentiment. It's not okay that you were abused. You got that? Let that statement sit with you for a moment. It sounds obvious, right? Of course it's not okay, but think about how you feel when you read that out loud. Do you believe for even half a millisecond that you caused the abuse? Throw that thought out the window right now. Stomp on it. Crush it. Never consider it again. Don't let anyone insinuate you did it. You did nothing wrong. To get better and face your abuse, you need to know without a doubt that you didn't cause it.

Abuse is not just sexual. Neglect is abuse. Children grow up with low self-worth. They parented themselves at a young age because their parents were addicts or mentally ill. Children who were slapped when they cried and told not to cry in public were abused. Silencing someone is abuse. These children went inside themselves, into the darkness, with all of their emotions. Like many people who come to AA with trauma, I had used alcohol to dull the pain and memories until it no longer worked.

Survivors tend to have selective memory because of the repressed abuse trauma, and that can still be true even when you have dislodged the secret. Holding this truth inside is painful, but I can assure you that your life will get better, and you will be able to make it through each day and see the heavy burden of your denial lift. A new you will emerge, one that you will enjoy getting to know.

UNDERSTANDING YOUR PAST

One of the first steps in recovery is understanding your past. There is so much that has been buried. Conversations, memories, and incidents will start to take on a different meaning now that you are aware of the abuse. It took years for me to unearth the specifics of my past, and I still don't understand a lot of it. But even though it is incredibly painful, looking back has helped me in my healing.

You can't get it all down in one pass, but over time you can assemble a bit of a narrative. Use my story as a template to fill in the details of your own story.

When did the abuse end?

My father's abuse ended when I was between the ages of eight and ten. I was angry, and my mother misunderstood my anger. I wish I could recall why I didn't tell anyone about the abuse, or why, if I did tell someone, they didn't speak up. I also wish I could remember more about how it felt or the intimacy I shared with my abuser, but much of it is a blur. Perhaps it is best that way, and what I know now—the undeniable fact that the abuse happened—is more than enough to set me on a path of healing.

Where did I grow up?

I was born and raised in a small town in Rhode Island. My mother had her own business selling international crafts and jewelry, and my father was an attorney. It was a time when kids in the neighborhood would play Kick the Can until dark on weekends, go to the beach in the summers, and eat homemade cookies at Christmas. I was raised Catholic-adjacent; I would go to church with my mom's parents until my grandma died of pancreatic cancer in her fifties. My parents became Bahá'í for a short period. Between these two religious paths, I have happy memories of spirituality and God through a community. Religion was a safe place where there would be no abuse, and I was less aware of my parents' tense marriage. My parents left the Bahá'í faith when I was seven, so God was no longer a presence in our home because we stopped going to church. My sister was born when I was eight, and I was not happy about it. I threw myself into horseback riding.

What did it feel like when the abuse ended?

I recall hot summer nights in New England after the abuse ended. I would lie in bed and stare at the ceiling, begging God to kill my parents. The abuse had come and gone, and I felt discarded. I would close my eyes and pray to be transported to the stars, far from this planet, high above this place. Then I would have a moment of morality or Catholic guilt and beg God to keep them alive. My survival instinct would kick in as I worried about my own care: Who would feed me and drive me to school if my parents were dead? Subconsciously, I began my plan to be independent as soon as possible.

What happened in my life that was particularly traumatic?

My parents divorced when I was thirteen. For as long as I can remember, they would argue in a bitter, biting way, with my dad shutting down emotionally, which would escalate my mother's ire. During that turbulent time, I remember being sent away for a weekend with my aunt and uncle in Martha's Vineyard because I had grown difficult for my mother to manage. She was extremely rigid in her parenting and rarely, if ever, affectionate. Her way of showing love was to decorate my room or force me to eat healthy food, insisting I thanked her for the spoonful of cod liver oil every morning. There was no penetrating her hard shell. I don't recall ever being kissed or hugged.

One of the issues of abuse is that no one knows what to look for. If it is a family legacy issue, they may be too busy denying their own abuse to laser in on why a preteen would be so angry. I did not have the capacity to explain that my father had done trust-shattering acts and then stopped when I was ten. He brought adult male love to my body and psyche when it wasn't formed. Then he took that love away, which launched a lifetime of black-and-white thinking with my romantic relationships. Everything in my relationships was a disaster, a tragedy, or the deepest love ever. I would over-modulate and under-modulate. I didn't understand until I was a grown woman that there was a second layer of the abuse cake: the gravity of a mother's betrayal or the impact of not being seen. Being told I had a problem with my attitude did not get to the root of the issue, but I also held on to the secret tight. We can protect our abusers and suffer gravely for it.

What were my teen years like?

During my junior year of high school, I had reached a breaking point with my mother's controlling ways, which was exacerbated by the fact that she was a single parent with two kids. So, I moved out of her house to live with my dad in an apartment down the road. I was drawn back subconsciously to the perpetrator, which led to a lifestyle of nonexistent parenting, subsisting on a diet of hot dogs and Dunkin' Donuts, and partying with a group of girlfriends on cheap Blue Nun white wine and mescaline, a hallucinogenic popular with young people at the time. I had lost any association with God and would struggle for decades to find my way back to spirituality. Drugs and alcohol numbed any memories, questions, or pain. I was lonely and didn't know that God could be accessed anywhere at any time. Later in life, after I faced the abuse, I had to contend with the idea that God witnessed the abuse and didn't stop it. I learned that God cannot stop people from doing horrible acts, but that he can be there in love and embodiment even when you can't see him.

What were my earliest romantic relationships like?

My confused little-girl-self grew to be a teen in a perpetual battle. *Don't dare cross me. I will destroy you.* A heat inside would rise up and boil over. I had fueled fights with boyfriends. When I was seventeen, I had a fight with a boyfriend who was a chef, and in a blind rage I grabbed his knife set from the back of his Jeep. He wrestled the knife out of my hand, but we had gotten cut up. When I returned home, I looked in the mirror at a drunken girl in a pink halter top that was streaked with blood. I was indignant, proud. *Take that,* I thought, as I crumpled up my once-favorite shirt and dumped it into the trash. I voraciously snorted cocaine until I couldn't feel my body parts, slept the weekends away, and failed school. I did what was necessary to not feel anxious when the loneliness took over.

What were the post-high school years like?

I was accepted to Emerson College (the only college I applied to) to study acting. I moved to Boston, knowing I had to work three jobs in order to make ends meet. My experience in Boston was great, but I never slept, and after my sophomore year, there was no more financial aid. I took six months off and moved back to my hometown and got a job as a waitress. My parents had mostly given up on me, but a guardian angel came in the form of a platonic friendship with a retired professor who saw a very dim light shining in me. He urged me to apply to more colleges where I could get financial aid. I enrolled at Canisius College in Buffalo, New York.

When I was in Buffalo, I couldn't get out of college fast enough. I was sick of juggling multiple jobs and schoolwork, so I took summer classes. I also had an internship at a media company, and the company chef referred me to an assistant job in New York City for a marketing executive in television. Again, another random angel working a miracle. I loved New York City, but I was a terrible secretary and never good at putting together presentations. Bless his heart, my boss never fired me. What I really wanted was to be in the movies, and I started to hang out with filmmakers. Escaping into fictional narratives was perfect for me to hide my truths. I gravitated to movie scripts that were about troubled people with drug or alcohol addiction and secrets. I felt like I was one of the characters, but I didn't know why.

What was my early career like?

I met my first husband, and we formed a production company to produce independent films. It was an exciting time for indie movies in New York City. As a producer, I rarely worked with women at my level. I would be in charge of a crew of 150 people and felt incredibly edgy and alone. I had no connection to the woman in my heart and my body, and I felt completely out of my element as a leader. *How did I get here?* I would think. I had a drive and a will, but I was scared of my own inner rage and lack of equilibrium with who I was. I ran from everyone because I felt so disconnected. I would write alone in a room for hours, but yet was profoundly disconnected to the truth.

When I was with people in my world professionally or personally, I created a lot of drama and confusion, which to me was connection. If I grew angry enough, I would see black. I raged at injustices and picked fights with my first husband that would start at sunup and drag on until dusk, leaving us both puffy and emotionally depleted. I rehashed how unfair my relationships were or how everyone misunderstood me. I was a convincing relentless debater, and I would win by simply having more fight in me. Then I would cave, feeling bad for being so abrasive, and beg for forgiveness. I was digging for answers in others rather than looking deep into the wound of betrayal inside my own heart.

Everything I did in my adult life was hard. My mind over-complicated things. I thought I had to jump through incredible hoops on fire to be accomplished and successful. I would make myself crazy with a level of perfectionism, and when I had a moment of clarity and self-preservation, I would alienate myself like I was a heartless monster. Eventually, my first marriage ended. What had brought us together in a shared love for cinema could not withstand his depression and my repressed pain and denial. We had a fairly amicable divorce, as there were little to no assets or children, via a worksheet filled out in a coffee shop. I recalled feeling sad, but I had also moved on to date my second husband. I didn't want time alone. On one hand, I should've taken time to explore the depths of myself, but that was a painful notion. I could not be alone with my feelings.

YOUR STORY

You don't need to do a deep dive into all the sections I provided above. Think about the moments in your life that resonate with you the most. I wrote in many journals for years and had countless therapy sessions to eventually streamline my narrative. The emotions that will come up with each question you ask about your past will be tied to the memories or anecdotes.

Take it slow and lean into your reactions. Rage can be our immediate reaction, which masks deep sorrow. When it comes to unpacking abuse, your history can be dark, but there is a significant amount of light. If you are recalling your past and it gets too intense, bring up a happy memory from that time to counterbalance the negative feelings.

When you understand your past, you can feel compassion and sympathy for yourself for as long as you need before you start to correct some of the behaviors that were part of your denial. A better life today in recovery can move fast, and then appear painfully slow. When the time comes, more will be revealed that will help you grow.

THOUGHT-PROVOKING QUESTIONS

What holds you back from looking deeper into your past? Are there family members who would be affected if you asked questions about areas of your past about which you need clarification?

How do you feel when other people describe their childhoods as idyllic? Do you feel like you were dealt a bad hand?

Are there any current aspects of your adult life that are carefree and child-like that reflect a time in your past when you were happy?

Chapter 3

FACING ABUSE

F acing abuse is brutal and painful. I am not going to sugarcoat it. When you finally decide to stare down your abuse and trauma head-on, you suddenly revert to being a young child about to acknowledge for the first time that your childhood was destroyed by an adult who couldn't keep their hands to themselves. The good news is that you are now an adult in control and can pull in the tools and understanding to pace your recovery. As the adult helping that young child facing the devastating truth, you can go as fast or slow as you like.

Sometimes facing the abuse in the first few weeks or months can feel like an altered reality. You may struggle to put a voice to the grim reality. This is a critical stage to continue speaking out and opening up through a trusted source. You can see a therapist or go to one of the many abuse support groups, such as Survivors of Incest Anonymous (SIA) (I went once, and it was game-changing to say the word *incest* out loud), Adult Survivors of Child Abuse (ASCA), or Sexual Assault Survivors Anonymous (SASA). You can also find someone within your religious organization, such as a pastor or a prayer group. You can tell a best friend or close confidant, but make sure the person will hold you accountable to your revelation in a loving way. I speak more about telling people and sharing your story in chapter 7.

YOUR RETURN TO DENIAL

It is important for survivors to be honest about being abused so that we can move on and live fulfilling, beautiful lives despite our past. You must own the facts of the abuse for you and your freedom. You may go through a period in your recovery where you feel victimized and like you received the short end of the stick. This may even make you question whether the assault actually occurred. I can assure you that going down this path is pointless. You are short-circuiting your life. The abuse cannot be taken back. It happened. There is no point in trying to be a sleuth. You now have choices to make with this new knowledge. Go within and discover more about yourself.

Doubts about whether the abuse memories were real arose as a defense mechanism against getting better. I also wondered if I made it up to attract attention in a dysfunctional way. As if something as horrible as incest would define me and make me unique. When I voiced my doubt, a wise person told me, "People generally don't use sexual abuse for popularity. So why would you do it?" Their assurance helped me go deeper into the depths of memory.

In 2014, I began attending AA meetings to get sober. But in 2018—six years since the abuse dream—I started having doubts. I asked my AA sponsor, "What if it isn't true? What if it's all just a fabrication of my mind?" I had fallen into a web of guilt. My dad was dead, and he couldn't defend himself if it was all a sham.

She took a fraction of a pause before asking, "What's not true? That your father molested you? Please."

She had witnessed many intimate parts of my recovery, and her affirmation of me kept me believing I was sane. If anyone heard me in my most raw and vulnerable moments, it was her.

Eventually, I discarded all theories of doubt. Every time I shared my abuse out loud, the shame had a little less power over me. I was abused, and I lived a painful life of isolation, aggression, lack of compassion, workaholism, lack of trust, and addiction until I confronted it. In order to face the truth in therapy, I had to be of one opinion: I had been abused. End of discussion. My father, one of my primary caretakers, had breached and violated his bond to me when I was a child. Because my trust had been shattered and contorted, I had been living an emotionally vague existence with people who thought they were close to me. I was a master of disguise. I wanted to have deeper relationships, but that involved reshaping my motives and my operating system. I would have to start trusting people.

Sexual abuse since infancy had instilled primal fears that sabotaged the development of my whole true essence. It all came down to first learning that I wasn't such a bad girl after all. I had a right to everything good in this world. Feeling equal to peers was one of the hardest tasks to unfold after accepting that I had been abused. I felt like an impostor, but I was a survivor.

Sexual abuse denial played a significant role in preventing me from achieving success in my career, choosing a life partner, or being a gentle, loving parent, but when I faced the truth, I was presented with all new options. I knew the truth about the abuse, and my task was to get well and stop all the behavior that prevented me from loving myself and those who loved me. Future failures could no longer be blamed on this earth-shattering, psyche-altering, trust-breaking breach of abuse. I had to rewire my thinking and rebuild my trust. I didn't want to be a victim.

I did not make perfect choices with men, money, or parenting right away, but with every week that passed, I witnessed learnings, discoveries, epiphanies, and miracles. I became more of the woman I could be and less of the woman I once was. I started to trust what the Universe was offering me, not as a failure or disappointment, but as an opportunity to live a little in the unknown without feeling threatened or scared. Every year, I made more life-affirming choices, such as taking my kids to

Europe, buying a house, expanding my business, and having a clearer vision of the type of life partner I was seeking. I would be stunned at the flexible and joyous way I would move through these levels. Don't assume you need a master plan. I didn't see these things as a possibility during my first few years of abuse recovery. There will come a day when you think, *Damn, I am awesome!* You will be dancing in the streets or speaking on a stage in front of hundreds of people. Or maybe you'll take a yoga class and smile because you have finally claimed your body as your own.

FINDING HOPE

In the beginning, some days are just hard. Even thinking about what you went through makes you sick to your stomach. You may question your faith or mute the truth with drugs or alcohol. You may alienate people who want to help you or overshare your truth in a business setting or on a first date. I am here to tell you that none of that matters right now. Stop judging yourself and start loving yourself. You have spent a lifetime denying the truth and preventing you from healing. The work you are about to do is not always linear or wrapped in a neat bow. It can be messy, and as you get to know the new you, surprises will come your way. The key is to stay hopeful, and if you don't know where to find hope, lean on others who have surmounted tragic times or difficulties. Listen to their stories. Find speakers who preach about the magic of recovery and their personal development. In order to find hope, you have to believe it is possible.

One of the ways I coped in my first year of recovery was becoming a student on the subject of recovery. Most books offer guidance on how to be a survivor of sexual abuse but not how to thrive in the history of sexual abuse. The writing felt archaic. Two prominent books written for sexual abuse survivors were published over twenty years ago. The books explained how to deal with a flashback, or a stressful situation that mirrored the vulnerability of abuse, or how to talk to a partner about sexual abuse. But they didn't address how to cope with life after sexual abuse denial. Facing my fighter self was part of the journey, but I wanted to learn new behaviors so she wouldn't stick around. She needed serious help to cope with the truth. I flipped through the books for chapters about thriving and living a beautiful life, but there were none. Where was the instruction booklet on what to do when I no longer wanted to die?

Where was the hope?

I wanted more than how-to tools for protection as I ventured out of my abused persona. As my self-love grew and I started to shed the shameful behaviors of an abused mentality, I sought literature about thriving and empowerment after abuse. The more I came out of my shell, I started to meet with and talk to amazing women, coaches, and entrepreneurs who were spreading their wings and achieving greatness despite their abusive background.

I learned about all kinds of abuse in my recovery research. I was part of a community that had been greatly silenced by our own shame. We have diminished our emotional abuse and taken on characteristics that mirror what had been done to us. Having hope is hard if we don't like the person who was shaped in reaction to the pain of abuse. Some survivors turn to promiscuity because they don't think there is hope for love, while some survivors have turned away from sexuality. It doesn't matter what form the abuse is; it all erodes the soul center so you can't tap into your sensuality and freedom to be an adult. Our journey to the center of our soul is where we rebuild. Your low self-worth is just a biproduct of what happened to you, so have hope that buried within is a magnificent creature ready to rise from the ashes.

One time, man approached me in an AA meeting after I shared

my story about my incestuous abuse. He sadly explained that he had been abused but couldn't tell his mom. He didn't have the courage to say it out loud to anyone, especially not to his parents, until he heard me share my story. He, like me, was in his forties. My story had given him hope to unveil his past and the pain. For him, facing abuse meant telling his mom, and he had been holding back on that piece for a long time. I urged him to address the secret because he had so much more living to do. He thanked me. I prayed for his healing.

The more you accept that the abuse happened to you, the more will be revealed about your true essence. While you are seeking to find the hidden person who has not yet grown out of the frightened, confused child you once were, you are ultimately looking for the good in all of this. It is there. It can be found.

FINDING HOPE MINDSETS

- Know that you did not cause the abuse. Ever. Ever. Never.

- Share your abuse out loud in safe spaces. It will lose its power over you every time you share it.

- Forgive yourself. When you look back at behavior where you may have felt crazy or were cruel with family members or friends, think about how it feels to be lied to and forgive yourself. Once you are on the path of healing, you will have time to explore and take ownership for certain behaviors.

- Discard doubt and explore recovery and your new way of living.

- Don't protect your abuser. They should have thought twice before committing an act of abuse. Your job right now is not to feel bad about their past or their mental illness. That forgiveness can come later if it is part of your journey.

YOUR EGO'S PART

Our ego is challenged when we face abuse. I have had countless conversations with survivors in recovery about how we have to smash our ego and why that is such a painful process. We leaned on our ego to create a false sense of self to protect ourselves from the truth. Self-preservation is a blessing and a curse when it comes to abuse. We have the capacity to handle the truth when we are ready, and in the initial stages of facing abuse, we almost have to battle against our own selves to recover. We have to prove to our damaged selves that we have the strength and resilience to grow and change without going crazy or feeling suicidal or depressed.

We all have our own ego, which can accentuate parts of our personality that prevent us from diving deeper into our memories. My ego was the driving force for my success, fame, and being the life of the party. Once I started to surrender to the facts of my denial, I had to tell my ego that I was now in charge and needed to be humble. I didn't have to exhibit certain characteristics that distracted me from healing. I needed to start tuning out the ego's voice and its commands for behavior that would create turmoil and distract me from getting better.

Many abuse survivors have low self-esteem, so it's ironic that they can also still be in a place of bravado. They leaned on a false sense of self in their survival. Their ego has kept them safe by directing the subconscious to a false power that manifests itself as dominance over others, manipulation, secrecy, addictive tendencies, and acting out for attention. When a survivor confronts their denial, the false self is revealed, and this can shatter their world. Our ego is scared the illusion that we are "fine" will be shattered because the outcome can be messy or unattractive when we face the truth. We could get painted in a less appealing light. When you stop deferring to your ego, you will learn intuitively what feels good rather than letting your ego do all the driving.

QUESTION YOUR ACTIONS

Facing your abuse allows you to pause and question your intentions behind your actions. Are your actions and motivations coming from a place of self-love or self-deprecation? Look at the past week and analyze your actions and motivations. Some areas of focus can be social, romance, finance, parenting, and friendships. For example:

- Did you go to that party to please others, or were you genuinely excited to socialize?

- Did you really want to break up with your boyfriend but couldn't because you were you afraid of conflict?

- Did you accept the job for less than you are worth because that has been the norm in the past? Were you afraid to ask for more money?

Our operating system was built on protection rather than being authentic and intimate with ourselves and others. In recovery, we can build a new operating system for ourselves.

Over time, we continue to face abuse in a nonlinear way. We initially face it and have to learn to live in our new truth. And then we go to new levels of facing the abuse as we heal and grow. Lightbulbs go off in our brain as we develop into our new selves. We step forward and then we can step back again. For me, it was important to be a student of the depths in which abuse affected me and understand the nuances of recovery beyond just taking long baths or accepting that this is my history and shouldering on.

In order for abuse recovery to be successful, I needed to focus on all areas that were depleted, but I couldn't do it all at once. Facing abuse is a process that happens over years depending on how deeply you want to vet it. Some days I'm really pissed and it sucks. I had been wronged and victimized. Adults I trusted should have shown me that the world was safe and good. Instead, they blurred it and darkened it for me, and when I went out into the bigger world to foster new relationships, I created a self I thought people would like. For the longest time, I thought I wasn't lucky because I would try for success and fail. But abuse has nothing to do with luck. People do shit to people, and it has an impact on how you interact with the real world as an adult. Your power is greater than your past. Be grateful that you are facing the facts, and then you can finally shape a life just for you.

THOUGHT-PROVOKING QUESTIONS

Are you still denying that you were abused?

Who was the first person you told about your abuse? If you haven't told anyone yet, explore why. Write about how you would feel, or how it felt, to "confess."

Where in your life did you experience deep denial versus acknowledgment of the abuse? Do you feel as if you have lost time? Take one event that occurred in your life, such as a divorce, job loss, or a conflict with a friend, and consider how repressed abuse could have played a role.

Did you have a special bond with your abuser? If your abuser was a parent, describe the special feelings about the bond despite the shame of it being connected to the abuse. Do you feel guilty that part of understanding your story is revealing they were the perpetrator in it?

Chapter 4

YOUR NEW VOICE

I f you have been screaming your entire life and are now in recovery from abuse denial, you can finally turn down the noise and hear your true self. It won't be sudden or easy. You have had one voice for a long time, and when you hear the new voice—soft, laughing, or comforting—tears will run down your face. You are exhausted because you've been screaming at people for so long in your justified rage and anger. My voice was loud before I faced abuse. I screamed a lot. I often screamed so loudly that I saw black. I raged and ravaged to justify my anger. I don't know how anyone put up with me.

Everyone has an inner voice. This voice takes on many different roles. At times, the inner voice will serve as your cheerleader, reminding you that you are doing well. Other times, the inner voice will warn you of impending danger or will tap into your intuitive nature and gut instincts. For many people, the inner voice is a trustworthy source of spirituality, logic, and reason. But for sexual abuse survivors, the inner voice can spiral into negative thoughts of self-deprecation, self-sabotage, and denial. It then becomes harder to filter out the negative, false thoughts. The inner voice has finally told you that you had been abused, but your ego is very crafty and will do everything in its power to prevent further harm, even if it means telling you that you are lying, fabricating stories, and that everyone will hate you. Your inner voice will chime back in and convince you that disclosing your abuse causes more problems rather than solving them. It will tell you to stop whining and just be happy like "normal" people.

It can be difficult to shut these critics off after years of denial and listening to the voice spew lies and the ego put up fences.

If you were not a screamer, you may have been quiet so you became a shell of yourself. The bad voice in your head threatens you with all kinds of fears every time you try to step out of your comfort zone. You may believe it is better to remain silent and blend into the background. The bad voices have hijacked the voice of your true self and told you not to expect to be anything special like those "normal people," no matter how you act out your denial and pain. Why should *you* expect to have a greatness others have? The negative voices are sinister and want you to fail.

One day you will realize you are different, but in a very magnificent way. You are a warrior. You will have a sword. You will use it in a strong way with love. You won't cut people down anymore because of your pain. But first, we need to find the good voice within you that has been buried in a blanket of abuse darkness.

THE VOICE OF ABUSE

The first step toward recovery from sexual abuse denial is acknowledging that you were violated. To live free of this secret is a herculean act in and of itself. But the challenging part is learning how to deal with your inner voice.

Abuse comes in many shapes and forms. The act may be brief, but it has long-term consequences for a child, a teenager, or an adult. Maybe someone in your life told you that you are worthless and disposable. Those harsh words are then imprinted in your brain, and you will begin to believe them about yourself. You no longer trust anyone because of what happened in your past. Whatever method you use to bury these feelings of inadequacy, chances are they are addictive, and you behave in ways that verify you are a "worthless piece of shit" (you aren't). Sexual abuse survivors are living the self-affirming prophecy bestowed upon them by their abuser, who was a self-absorbed narcissistic sicko. The lie you have been telling yourself for so long—that the abuse never happened—becomes a reality. This lie falsely justifies your behaviors as an addict, a mean person, or feeling depressed. You may think you are a bad person because you exhibit such toxic behavior. You live outside of yourself because there is such deep, traumatic pain within, and tapping into it would feel like death. But the truth of freedom is within you.

For a long time in my recovery, I struggled to identify when my voice was reflecting the pain of abuse or speaking up as a survivor. Either way, I would tell the voice that I was in charge and that I intended to keep moving forward. Once you understand the darker voices and continue to fight them, they will quiet down. They are pathetically weak when they smell victory.

I used to have intrusive thoughts that my ex-husband would be castrated or that my children would be harmed. I screamed, then I numbed, and then I healed, and the cycle repeated itself. For many years, I had no therapy or recovery, and my only solace was facials, a large pitcher of gin gimlets, and watching episodes of *So You Think You Can Dance*. If you knew me now, you would be shocked to learn that was once my reality. I once fought so hard with my ex-husband that I called the police on myself because I was afraid of my own rage. When the police arrived, they assumed I had reported my ex-husband for domestic violence. I will never forget his down-turned face, the scratches on his cheeks, and his ripped shirt as the officers gave him the riot act. But I was the one who was violent and angry. Yes, it takes two to tango, and my ex was far from a saint, but I was a voracious yeller who wanted to crush and destroy. On the inside, I was an angry, violent ten-year-old.

There was a shred of something inside of me that believed I

wasn't an angry person, but then I would be furious and violent, and I'd feel hopeless. I couldn't quite pinpoint what was wrong. I wish I had a voice to tell people, "I think there is something very wrong with me," and to seek help for trauma. Yet, *trauma* was not a word anyone said in my family or in my marriage. Every now and then, I would get a glimmer that I was good and lovely, and I would go out of my way for my spouse, my kids, and my friends. I would feel intelligent, productive, and well-mannered. I would be fashionable and have shiny hair. I would wash my car and fly to Maui for a dream holiday. But still . . . there are the negative voices. And they would win. Nothing good would last for long.

After my dream, I wanted to turn my life around right away by remembering the abuse, but the flashbacks and more memories did not come immediately. My inner psyche was still protecting me from knowing too much about the abuse history, and my ego kept me drinking for a little while longer so I wouldn't get overwhelmed. The dream and the realization of abuse pack a power punch. The specifics of the abuse never became clear in the years that followed. We can handle only what our emotional maturity level can take and what will serve us. Even now, I have a sense of what else could have happened based on what I feel in my body. Being a mature adult woman who makes strong and powerful personal sexual choices no longer terrorizes me.

GRIEVING A LOST VOICE

There are always past patterns we can trace back and mourn that we didn't recognize our pain and desire to speak out sooner. We have to process the grief of not having a voice. In my twenties, I screamed with oil pastels on large artist pads. My mom, ironically, had suggested it because she was studying to be an art therapist. The drawings only added to my confusion. I would look at what

I created on those pads—intercrossing coils of red and black chaos and flowers staggering to grow under the weight of heavy octagonal shapes—and inside me something would think, *Girl, you have major problems.* The images screamed for analysis, but no one around me detected anything dark or secretive in my history. So I just thought I had a really messed-up mind. I didn't speak about why I would be drawing in this way. I just thought it was something angry people did.

Since I was a child, I had either apologized for my voice or had been fueled by its rage. When I was a little girl, I would mouth off, refuse to practice piano, or would be mean to my little sister. I had to write perfect "I'm sorry for my behavior" notes to my mother in order to be let out of my room. One time when I was an adult, my mom visited me in Los Angeles, and she was upset with my youngest child's behavior. She made my daughter sit alone in her room and write an "I am sorry" note. I was livid. I couldn't support that kind of shameful punishing.

"Never force her do that again," I seethed.

When I finally faced the abuse, I didn't confront my mother about it until two years later. As an adult, I was so scared to speak up to her. I was still convinced the abuse was somehow my fault and that she wouldn't believe me. I needed a time-out, a break, and I didn't care if it was for a lifetime. I didn't want to be silenced on another level of denial any longer. I had outgrown that little girl and was no longer writing "I am sorry" notes.

It would be an understatement to say that learning you have been sexually abused is devastating. Facing the abuse in midlife caused an enormous upheaval for me because it forced me to question how I had operated for forty-three years without knowing. I started to say "no" with my recovered voice because I finally had choices. I heard "me" speaking—someone I had never met before—and I was astounded.

It was not okay to be sexually abused, and we need to use our voice to talk about that first and foremost. The rest of the world can wait. My world did not begin until I finally said "yes" to accepting the truth of the abuse and the memories that my mind had chosen to bury. I was developing defense mechanisms against the negative voices as I mourned all the ways I had not spoken up when I was treated without dignity (e.g., sleeping with men who didn't love me, or accepting low pay for employment).

Even as I sat down to write this book, before my butt even hit the chair, the voice in my head would say, "You're fat. Who do you think you are writing a book that will never amount to anything or mean anything to anyone when you should be working on making yourself more beautiful? You need to be more beautiful for anyone to love you." Or the voice would say, "You have crappy clothes and no self-image. You are poor and frumpy."

That voice is demonizing. It is a bad voice. It distracts me from my goals. It doesn't want me to get better or to help others. It wants to distract me with my messy desk or my meowing cat. It wants me to misinterpret and obsess over something a guy I am dating might have said so that I could go on a three-day emotional bender followed by a two-day emotional hangover. The voices demand I listen to them, but I don't want to listen to them any longer.

It's not worth it to hold it all inside. Those bad voices will kill you. You have to take action in recovery, even if it means leaving some tread marks behind.

TAKE ACTION WITH YOUR VOICE

In the early stages of recovery, I often lacked succinct words to express how I felt. I couldn't even tap into writing, which was the modality I'd relied on throughout all those years. Instead, I would grab a pen and a notebook and let my hand angrily scribble on the pages.

This is a good exercise for when you want to really tap into that deep subconscious voice. But it only works when you don't think about it, so you have to be willing to allow your narrative to make little to no sense. You also need to be fearless about what you say. You can tap into deeply lodged emotions or bad voices, but now you get to be in charge of that voice.

- Sit in a quiet space with a pen and paper.

- Write without thinking. Let yourself feel possessed. Let tears stream down your face or burst into laughter. Don't hide from your emotions.

- Now take the pen in your nondominant hand. Write without thinking. Write down any words that come to mind. For example, *ouch*, *pain*, *Daddy*, *hate*, *hell*.

It doesn't matter if you can't read what you wrote. Just scrawl and rip and vomit onto the page all those repressed thoughts the bad voice has been whispering in your ear. Then rip that paper to shreds and destroy those dark, scrawling, uncontrolled scratches.

Feel yourself coming alive. The real you is taking flight.

CHOICE OVER YOUR VOICE

For nearly four decades, my sexual abuse at such a young age influenced so much of what I said and did. I have listened to women share in twelve-step meetings that they assumed they were promiscuous because they had been taken advantage of at a young age. They had spent their entire lives giving themselves and their souls away with sex. "Slut," the voices said. But the voices are lying. These women had been exploited by an adult who should have known better, and the abuse has altered their self-persona forever.

If you are reading this book, then it is safe to assume that you or someone you love endured sexual, emotional, or physical abuse as a child. There is a pervasive sense of shame that we were somehow responsible for the sexual abuse, and worst of all, that we liked it! So I'll say this again, because I had to hear it a lot of times:

You did not cause sexual abuse or any other kind of abuse. You get to talk about it and choose how you remember, share, and heal.

When the bad voice and my ego knew I was getting better, they introduced me to the concept that the abuse did something for me as a child and that I "liked" it. That left me emotionally shaken for at least a week. *How could I have liked it?* My stomach turned just thinking about it. But, thankfully, I had a therapist who helped me understand that receiving affection from my father when I was a young girl was a natural yearning. How was I to know he'd gone too far? Who was I comparing it to? It's not like I went to second grade and asked one of my classmates, "So, is it normal for your father to stroke you all over when you are naked?"

As if enduring a lifetime with a damaged and misaligned soul that was slowly dying beneath all the dark shame wasn't bad enough, the bad voices made me loathe myself in a new way once I was in recovery. The bad voices continued to tell me shameful things about myself. At AA meetings, I have heard beautiful women say, "I disgust myself. I was sexually abused, and I know it probably plays a part, but I just hate myself." *Probably?* I can assure you the sexual abuse has everything to do with your self-loathing.

For a long time, I didn't fight against the bad voices until

I developed my self-worth and self-esteem. Then I knew they were full of crap because I started to accumulate evidence that I was a good person. Each new action built the new voice inside of me—being a secretary for an AA meeting, being a substitute teacher, telling someone I was uncomfortable in a relationship, or expressing that I didn't like how someone in authority treated me. This new voice was unique to the woman I was becoming. I started seeing patterns of what I liked and didn't like. I found I was charitable and could organize Secret Santa for kids who wrote letters to the post office with their Christmas wishes every year. When I co-parented our children, I could be okay if I couldn't agree with my ex-husband. I discovered a new strength within myself each time I communicated in a firm and steady voice rather than screaming.

BAD VOICE VERSUS GOOD VOICE

It can be difficult to distinguish between the good voice that wants to be productive and helpful, and the bad voice that wants to cause us harm and pain. This can be especially challenging when we are in the process of healing. So, how can you tell the difference between the bad voice's overanalyzing chatter and the proactive and purposeful good voice? When I find solutions to my problems in a peaceful and nonurgent state of being, I am being driven by the good voice. When I am swashbuckling my way through a situation, I am usually just trying to drown out the bad voices of suspicion and distrust.

Our thoughts are like runaway trains that prompt the desire to run into escapism or engage in fight-or-flight reactions. We have to give a good voice to our newly emerging selves by constantly speaking about our big goals and life dreams. We must also be open to witnessing the evidence (miracles) that can happen in our life. We need to silence the critical voices in our heads so we can discern what we are truly called to do or be. So how can we practice thought vigilance? Here a few steps to get you started:

- Don't beat yourself up. If you are not sure of your next strategic move, stay silent and steady until you do, and don't get impatient. You're going through inner healing, which will prepare you for an easier, softer approach.

- Talk to the bad voices. Tell them to shut up. You are not interested in what they are saying.

- Put sticky notes around your house with life-affirming messages written on them, such as "I love you" or "I am safe."

- Repeat "I am safe" over and over, even if your body doesn't believe you.

Our bad voices speak the loudest in the areas where we suffer the most: low self-esteem, low self-confidence, and trusting people. Remember that you are your voices, so you get to choose which one you listen to during your recovery.

You need to stop entertaining the bad voice and move your narrative into a more productive, kinder good voice. When you listen to the good voice, it creates more trust in yourself.

Are you aware of when you intentionally allow the bad voice to push you and create negative talk? For example, do you notice a lot of negative self-talk in areas such as your relationships, body image, or how you do business? Behind the bad voices are fear, and often it is imagined. Once we understand what we are afraid of, we can use a good voice to give ourselves love and understanding, as well as lead us to a more productive tangible solution. The goal is to practice more consciousness in reality than in denial, which is fueled by fear.

Let's look at the following examples:

Business

Bad voice: None of the women in this networking group care about me. I don't make as much money as them, my clothes aren't as nice, and I bet none of them were abused.

Is this real or imagined? Imagined. I don't know any of these women.

Good voice: These women are so lovely. I can't wait to get to know them. We are all unique in our own way. I wonder what I can do to help in the organization to support them better.

Money

Bad voice: If I don't make a sale soon, I could be close to poverty.

Is this real or imagined? Imagined. I am nowhere close to living in my car.

Good voice: You have money in your account, have a few job opportunities, and friends who would help you out in a pinch before it came to dire poverty. Who would you like to work with if you could attract your ideal client today?

Now it's your turn. Make a list of five categories in your life where the bad voice takes control. Then choose the top three categories where you hear the bad voice the most and identify whether the fear is real or imaged. Then counter the bad voice with the good voice. Repeat this exercise every day to actively change your thinking.

THE VOICE OF THE HEART

Wherever you are in your recovery from abuse denial, the more you can tap into your *heart brain* rather than your *thinking brain*, the better. This is a gradual process that begins with meditation and becoming comfortable in silence. I have done open-eye meditations when it felt like my heart burst open when the instructor and I locked gazes. Nature encounters, such as seeing a deer or a hummingbird, have taken me out of my head and into my heart. Any connection I make with the goodness around me takes me outside of my head and into the present.

Your heart knows what is best as it heals. You can smile when you listen to your heart. You can write. You can breathe. You can love. You may hear voices, but you will have the tools to deal with them in a healthy manner. Can you imagine living a life without the negative voices? Wow, what a novel idea.

When we listen to our heart and talk to ourselves gently, we will attract people in our lives who live on the same vibrational platform. Be brave and unflappable in your destiny as a survivor. Don't cower in any more shame. When we start to make decisions from our heart space, we may feel as if we are swimming against the stream. I made decisions that were not the popular opinion, but I felt in my heart it was right. Some of those decisions may not have been the fastest or best paths to my goals, but they were the best lessons for me. We are going to struggle in recovery. I would be lying if I said we come out on the other side "all better." The more you tap into that voice that comes from the heart—even if it is uncomfortable to make a decision that goes against the grain—trust that it is coming from a voice you can rely on. While your mind may play tricks on you, your heart never lies.

As you use your new voice from your heart space, you are going to take new risks, and people may not love what you have to say. Just know that this is all a learning process. Make new choices next time. Lean in to your heart space to determine whether you need to evaluate your communication, or if you need to set a powerful boundary that someone may not like. You are doing it as the new you!

THOUGHT-PROVOKING QUESTIONS

Which voices are stronger for you: the good voices or bad voices? Take note of the dialogue between your good and bad voices. Good voices are quiet and soft, and they say things like, "That felt nice to spend time with that person," or, "I did a good job finishing that task." Bad voices will latch onto the tail end of these thoughts and try to discount them.

Has your voice sounded different in recovery? Have you ever stopped and thought to yourself, "I said that"? Write about a time when you stood up for yourself and heard your voice in a new way.

What modes do you use to express yourself? Are you an artist or a musician? Consider ways you can incorporate a voice of recovery into your art.

Chapter 5

FIGHT OR FLIGHT

When you are in recovery from abuse denial, you will step into new areas of your life and face challenges and growth. While this can be good news, as survivors start to see paths of success and emotional freedom, what can arise in tandem is panic, anxiety, or other coping mechanisms and disorders. These painful conditions may be triggered by stepping into areas of growth and expansion but also body memories. When faced with conflict, both real and historical, your body will create new signals to indicate you are not safe. The goal is to learn how to manage these reactions and teach your body that you are now in the driver's seat and in charge of your circumstances.

Panic and anxiety can sometimes unlock new memories and flashbacks. One day in the midst of a panic attack, I was transported back to my little-girl body where the abuse took place. The feelings causing my adult panic were unmistakably hers. *Would it be tonight,* I had thought. The childhood bed was large and wide and long, and I almost didn't feel like my body was in it or a ghost of myself was there. I left my body and observed whenever my dad opened that bedroom door. Reliving that experience as an adult caused a weird sensation across my cheekbones, and the skin and blood beneath became cold as if kissed by dry ice. When I later wrote down my experience, my jaw locked and it felt like something had punched in my heart. I rocked in bed to ground myself, to remind myself that I was an adult, but to also stay present to see what I could learn about my abused child.

While you are processing, accepting, and understanding your trauma, you are teaching your body that perceived breaches of trust aren't always so cut-and-dried. I know how painful and hard that process can be. I wish I could make it better for you, but I can assure you that you can have fewer stressful moments if you are vigilant about your thoughts and are conscious of your body and breath.

My recovery uncovered many issues that manifested as panic attacks, but my mind also perceived threats that were not real but based on old messaging, such as I was bad or was doing something wrong. Everyone's recovery will be different. Whatever you are going through, ask a lot of questions and trust your body and mind, which are now emerging as unique to your true self outside of the abuse denial. You are worth it.

I understand that not everyone experiences panic attacks, but the survival instinct of fight or flight is real. The fight-or-flight response is "a physiological reaction that occurs in response to a perceived harmful event, attack, or threat to survival."[2] When we experienced sexual assault and trauma, we went into the fight-or-flight cycle, but we often had to freeze because it was impossible to fight. We have the body memory of the abuse, which can be triggered by a present-day threat that is psychological (both real or imagined), and we freeze up. "The freeze response, unlike fight or flight, is considered an 'I can't' response and occurs when the body is overwhelmed."[3] The breach of trust for survivors activates fight or flight on a deep level when trust is questioned, which can be frequent and continuous in the early years of recovery.

---

[2] "Fight-or-flight response," Wikipedia, last modified October 8, 2022, https://en.wikipedia.org/wiki/Fight-or-flight_response#cite_note-Cannon_-_Fight_or_Flight_Response-1.

[3] "Responses," Survivors Voices, accessed November 4, 2022, https://survivorsvoices.ca/responses/.

PANIC ATTACKS

My full-blown panic attacks began in 2013, a year after my abuse dream. They came on slowly at first, then more frequently. The truth is the panic attacks almost killed me more than facing the truth about my sexual abuse. While they were an important part of my body and mind waking up, they were the most terrifying, debilitating incarnations of near-death in my lifetime

The panic attacks would occur weekly without rational provocation for years, and they still occur monthly to this day. The difference is that I have learned how to deal with them in a healthier way. Have you ever had a chest-crushing, choking, phlegm-inducing panic attack? I don't want to discourage you by saying they may never go away, but I can help you to understand how to manage them and learn more about the inner scars that abuse has left on your psyche.

Coping with Fight or Flight

Often when I was in the grip of a brutal panic attack, I thought denial would have been preferable! I assure you, despite feeling punished and discouraged, there is relief in recovery around the corner. Eventually, my panic attacks became less frequent as I strengthened my belief that I deserve love and am loved.

My panic attacks were caused by the fear that I had done something wrong, misjudged a situation, or made the wrong choice. The attack served as both a messenger and an assailant. It came swooping in to remind me, "Girl, stop thinking so bad about yourself!" In the early days, I interpreted the attacks as my inner spirit warning me that I was letting the dark, doubtful voices to enter. I needed to repeat the mantra: *I am safe. I am safe. I am safe.* Now when I have a panic attack, I know it means

I've lost control of myself, so I'll say, "I am strong. I am strong. I am strong." That took six years to develop.

A mini version of the attacks began in early 2012, six months before I woke up from the abuse dream. I had quit smoking pot for the first time since I started at the age of thirteen. The change cleared the neural pathways in my brain, and new pistons that had previously been dulled by marijuana began firing every minute. I was more alert and in the present moment. I assumed the anxious feeling that made my chest hurt and my throat close up was caused by my decision to stop smoking marijuana. I had no idea these symptoms were related to abuse that had been suppressed.

In January of 2013, one month after having the abuse dream, I started working as a cashier at Trader Joe's. This job, which lasted six months, was part of my spiritual reboot. Even though it didn't make much financial sense at $11 an hour, its rigor and simplicity set the stage for me to face the abuse. Trader Joe's provided me with the perfect safe haven during my second divorce and the end of the film career that had been my identity for decades. The Universe was definitely aligned for this safe landing, because the day I walked into the Westwood Village store, a manager immediately gave me a job, despite the fact that others had told me it was impossible to get hired there. I was even given a special work schedule so I could still pick up my two small children from their different schools.

For eight hours a day, people only knew me as Kim the Clerk. I would have horrendous panic attacks while working the cash register during peak hours—a full exposure of self. Every week, without warning, I had to grab a friend to cover the register so I could just die in the bathroom, begging God to make it stop as tears streamed down my face.

The truth was, I wasn't an anxious person. I was in a panic.

My body was stuck in fight-or-flight mode. I had a lot of frozen memories because I wasn't able to react or seek recourse when I was a child. I was having panic attacks on a weekly basis.

I had no idea who I was in what felt like a broken body that was revolting against me. My therapist was helping me scratch the surface of the primal reactions to facing abuse: the body memories, flashbacks, and panic. In that first year, she didn't diagnose me with a disorder because everything was too new, fresh, and intense to label. I didn't know how to deal with the fact that I had been abused while also going about my daily life. Aside from when I wanted to flee the perceived dangers in my mind, working at Trader Joe's and getting my own apartment after my divorce gave me new footing in my personal quest to discover who I really was.

I thought the hour-long panic attacks were going to kill me. They were debilitating. Bone crushing. The attack would rip through me bit by bit, and I would pray as my teeth ached that my heart wouldn't go into full arrest. I was transported to that same precipice as a small child being violated by a grown man who was my dear daddy. My throat would ache, raw and hot. I would scream into a pillow, but it didn't work on those panic attacks. Screaming under water in a bathtub did not derail their descent.

If you are having panic attacks that feel like you are being punished, or if you don't think you will get through the pain, remember that as we recover, we start to learn to manage our minds. You are peeling back some of the first most painful layers of denial from the abuse. These early stages will be shocking and painful, but I assure you, it's the gateway to a much better life. Later in this book, I explore thought vigilance and body love, both of which are essential to keeping us calm and centered. For right now, just breathe, trust in yourself, and know you are on the right path to recovery.

SPIRITUALITY IN THE FIGHT OR FLIGHT

In 2016, my second year of sobriety, I was in a good place working as a substitute teacher at my children's school and earning an honest wage. Passing the CBEST exam to become a substitute was one of the most grueling academic endeavors I had faced since college. I studied my ass off, relearning sixth-grade math. After failing all the practice tests, I had a moment with God in the exam room. Through AA, I had found a new connection with a God of my understanding (which was still a fickle relationship), so I leaned on this spiritual construct. I needed some force other than myself to partner with me in my vulnerable fear at that time.

"God, I have failed all the practice tests. I could fail this exam. If you want me to be a substitute teacher, you will help me pass. If you don't, then I will fail, and I am fine with that."

I passed with high marks and received my certification.

Substitute teaching for kindergarten was a saving grace. I had a new sense of compassion for what my own children experienced all day: the grind of elementary public school. It really brought me closer to their experience. I was on the path of recovery, and the panic attacks had died down for a little while. I was deepening my relationship with a God I now understood was my partner, and the rest of the way was up. No more hold-ups. Life would skyrocket.

Then, at the time, a new boyfriend suddenly dumped me by email because his life was too chaotic to have me in it. This was also my first sober relationship, so there was no drugs or alcohol to quell my despair. I was stunned after reading his email. I felt nothing. I flatlined my feelings, but I couldn't keep that up for long. I was plunged into bouts of the most ferocious panic attacks I had ever experienced. This level of love, still formative, brought on the mother lode of pain. I had trusted, and that trust had been breached. I had been abandoned and left to suffer with my wounds ripped open. I had nowhere to run from the emotional pain, so it just did a number on my body.

The panic attacks came in waves for several days after that. They struck seemingly unprovoked when I was standing in front of the little kids in the classroom. It felt like a thumb was pressing on my throat, strangling me. I couldn't breathe, I couldn't swallow, and all I could think about was the chest-crushing pressure and how I was going to die. Yet, I was so good at putting on a game face even though I was in so much pain and could barely make it through the day. If there had been a wine bottle lying around, I would have ripped out the cork and downed as much as possible to make this feeling go away. Fortunately, there was no alcohol in the kindergarten classroom.

During my lunch break, I prayed to God to help me through this. I used to pray to God in the same way when I was a child. This was childhood panic that had been dormant and squashed. I wasn't a helpless child anymore. I had children of my own. I needed to take back my life. No man was going to take that from me. I also realized that my only connection with God was when I wanted something or to be saved, and I wanted to change that. It had to be pervading and constant.

A few nights later, I was having a whopper panic attack and reached out to a woman in AA who had a strong spiritual program in place for dealing with anxiety.

"Your throat is not going to close up permanently. You're not going to die. You need to breathe," she said, and then she took ten long breaths with me. No one in my life had ever taken a breath with me before.

As I calmed down, we talked about accepting my feelings, how they were not going to actually kill me if I felt them and walked through them. I wondered how my life would be if I could be bigger than my fear. If I was always going to have panic attacks when it came to emotional intimacy, I could no longer fight or fear my feelings. I wanted to stand up to the voice— the panic voice, the mean voice. I even ventured to say the voice was the devil. I didn't want to scream and yell senselessly at the people I loved anymore, but I had permission to be brutal with the voice that caused my panic. *Shut up, motherfucker,* I told the voice. *There is no room for you in my life anymore. You are not my God. You are the devil. I won't believe in you anymore.*

My friend then texted me a Bible quote: "Do not be anxious about anything, but in every situation, by prayer and petition, with thanksgiving [say it, ask for it, and be in gratitude], present your requests to God. And the peace of God, which transcends all understanding, will guard your hearts and your minds in Christ Jesus" (Philippians 4:6–7, New International Version).

She also sent me this beautiful meditation about owning the protection of your spirit:

> I will be more afraid of spirit-unrest, of soul-disturbance, or any ruffling of the mind, than of earthquake or fire. When I feel the calm of my spirit has been broken by emotional upset, then I must steal away alone with God, until my heart sings and all is strong and calm again. Uncalm times are the only times when evil can find an entrance. I will beware of unguarded spots of unrest. I will try to keep calm, no matter what turmoil surrounds me.[4]

While anxiety and panic attacks are painful side effects of recovery and a new sense of self-awareness, they allow us to strengthen our spiritual program and connect with other survivors who are also in the same situation. You get to build a

---

[4] *Twenty-Four Hours a Day* (Center City: Hazelden Publishing, 2019), 21.

tribe of spiritual warriors so you never feel alone. You also get an opportunity to lean into your faith. During my early recovery, I had a lot of issues with God because I still felt he was doing this to my life in some way. I prayed like a crazy person to God when I was in the throes of attacks. I may have prayed really hard to God when I was being abused too. He was listening, but it's impossible for a child to understand that God still exists when the traumatic act doesn't stop. My whole life, my relationship with God was based on bargaining: give me this and I will be good. But I was already perfect in God's eyes. There was no good or bad. He just wanted me to feel loved.

If you are currently experiencing panic or anxiety attacks, I know how difficult it may be to appreciate them or feel like they have anything to do with your spiritual journey. Trust me, I did not appreciate them at all after two years of constant attacks. At the time of this writing, eight years later, I still have anxiety attacks, though less frequently. I have to move forward based on the intuitive guidance of my heart and my experiences with God in the stillness.

BEING HONEST ABOUT PANIC AND ANXIETY

The panic attacks went away again for a few months in 2017. I was five years into recovering from denial of abuse and fell into thinking it was possible they were gone forever. Then, one Saturday morning, I had a panic attack that floored me. I had let the old thoughts of a scared, damaged woman infiltrate my beautiful Saturday morning. I had lost faith in the spiritual path that brought me here, and I was now spiraling out in a place of loneliness and lack of love. Many sexual abuse survivors believe they are terminally alone due to the nastiness of their secrets, and they block themselves from connecting with others.

I used to hide in shame from the panic attacks, especially from my children, who were twelve and eight at the time. I would distract them with the TV, then go into my room and hold myself and shake. This time, I was not interested in hiding. I slid down the side of my bed, allowing the tears to stream down my cheeks. I prayed to God for the strength to no longer hide my brokenness behind my healing. But I couldn't tell my kids I was having a panic attack because of sexual abuse recovery—they were too young, and I had to appear "human" and fallible. When my kids found me, I told them in a safe and loving way that I was okay and just having feelings. I was demonstrating to them that it was okay to be a fully human mommy in front of them. I was not some damaged harlot of hell. I was a woman trying to get back on her feet and to live her biggest dreams after coping with sexual abuse. It all moved too fast sometimes, and I had to slow down.

I told them my chest hurt but that it would pass. They brought me water and tissues, and they smoothed my hair. They were obviously concerned, but I showed them in a safe, sane way that adults have vulnerable moments. After I recovered, I was overcome with complete joy. We went to the farmers' market in the sun, where we bought avocados and goat cheese, and then went to Stone Candle, my favorite candle store in Los Angeles. The owner had an ice cream cooler, and the girls ate free ice cream sandwiches at ten in the morning. We smelled candles and infused oils for our burner at home. It was like the sunrise after the perfect storm.

While it was the abuse that caused my panic attacks, it was the most organic way for me to show my kids that it's okay to be their fullest messy selves. These were the miraculous and spiritual moments that resulted from the panic attacks. When my children had feelings or were anxious, how could I tell them they didn't have the right to stand in their own discomforts and power after they witnessed my discomfort?

The best part was that I wasn't angry that this random panic attack happened after not having any for so long. Instead, I was so grateful that my body and mind were able to show me that I was out of spiritual and creative alignment with the rest of my beautiful life. *You have gotten ahead of yourself in your head*, I was warned. I would need to be on vigilant patrol at all times to prevent my mind from hijacking itself. That is the gateway to panic attacks. When I am running too fast and too hard, I am not fully present in the midst of my life's miracles.

JUST BREATHE

Breath is life. Breathing helps us battle panic, anxiety, or fear in the moment and keeps us grounded in the present. Breathing can slow down our heart, which helps us feel calmer. Breathing will also help you battle self-judgment, which is a preventive practice to keep the attacks at bay.

Panic attacks are no laughing matter, and it can feel like they will kill you, but you can stretch to new levels of self-preservation and recovery if you allow yourself to listen to their message.

Here are a few strategies for dealing with panic attacks. As always, seek counseling if your panic attacks are debilitating. I was taught a valuable breathing exercise by shamanic healers that has helped me in many situations.

Try this breathing exercise the next time you are having a panic attack or when the bad voices are screaming at you. You can practice this breathing exercise when you are standing, but it is best if you are sitting because you are more grounded. You can do it with your eyes open or closed.

- Turn your head to your left and breathe in while counting to thirteen.

- Turn your head to your right and exhale to the count of thirteen, making space for all that is beautiful and positive in your life to come in. You can make a mental list in the moment based on what comes to you.

- Then, as you breathe in again to the count of thirteen, gather up all the negativity in your life.

- Look to the left and exhale to the count of thirteen, breathing out these negative, troubling thoughts.

- Repeat the cycle twelve more times.

I have practiced this breathing exercise in public places, like when I was getting my oil changed in Jiffy Lube, but it works and no one really notices. I can't say it takes away the reverberations, which still crackle around in my system for the next twenty-four hours, but the whopper of a panic attack is diffused in the moment.

You will normalize. It will happen. It happened to me. I am fantastic and realized in my fullest self. What you go through in the process of getting to the other side creates a love and an awareness in your heart that will bring new tears to your eyes. Tears of love, happiness, and whole connection.

As you breathe, understand that you have the right to reclaim your soul and realign your body to the person you were born to be. To do so, you will strive to reclaim your body as your own, free of the memories of abuse. You can heal your soul with your higher source and with rigorous focus on your thoughts and your breath. God bless you and keep you safe and warm.

JUDGMENT AND COMPARISON

My relationship with panic attacks is unique because they reveal areas where I am ignoring my self-love. The panic is caused by fear. During my attacks, the negative voices judge me and say, *You are going to pay for that one, Kim. You were bad.* Then my mind compares me to all the less-broken people in the world who are happy and healed. The attacks are fueled by this worrying thought process, or if I judge myself for a decision I made or something I said. When I doubt the present as it unfolds, I don't trust that each of my experiences will teach me something about my life and offer me growth. Therefore, I have to be in a constant state of self-love so I can operate from a decent, healthy place. Life can be challenging, causing people to trip up, and I get tripped up too.

How can we identify self-judgment? Try these three tips to bring yourself closer to self-love.

Stop negative self-judgment

Get curious about your panic and anxiety. How do you negatively judge yourself? Did you fall short of a goal you set for yourself? Are you comparing yourself to someone you consider to be "healthier" or "saner" than you?

Stay focused

Focus on what you are doing well in recovery. Before you go to bed each night, think about all of your wins. When you focus on the positive moments of your day, the negative energy dissipates, as do the chances of having a panic or anxiety attack.

Stay active

While meditation can help us to deepen our awareness, too much silence can amplify the negative voices in our head. Play loud music, dance around, or go to a concert or a place where there is activity. A free outdoor concert, a busy café, an action film . . . anything to trip up the voices. You don't have to stay long. You can be in control of your regulation.

When we start to believe we are all alone in the world, our old programming from the past can rule us. Your nervous system freaks the hell out! Hopefully, you will get to a place where you love the unique you so much that you can't imagine comparing yourself to someone else and then judging how you are imperfect. You are not perfect—no one is—but you need to give yourself some grace.

THOUGHT-PROVOKING QUESTIONS

Have you told anyone about your panic or anxiety attacks? Sharing a detailed account with someone can take away the secret and shame.

What is the story you are telling yourself when you go into fight, flight, or freeze mode? How can you change your messaging to yourself with less judgment?

If you don't suffer from anxiety or depression, do you repress your feelings in anger or silence? Do you feel obligated to hide these coping mechanisms from those you love?

What debilitating behavior in your recovery path went away for a while and then came back? How did you handle its return? How was it different, and how can you use that as a learning tool?

Chapter 6
THERAPY

Therapy is helpful when you are in recovery from sexual abuse denial. Some therapists are perfect partners for a safe landing no matter how we arrive. Others may not be a good fit depending on your maturity level and willingness to open up. Because we enter recovery vulnerable and frightened, it is necessary to feel safe with someone so you can allow your darkest, saddest self to emerge in these sessions. It is important to understand that your therapy sessions plant the seeds, and you will continue to heal long after you leave the room.

My initial dream of abuse prompted me to call my ex-marriage counselor, who then referred me to Rena, the therapist who would change my life. While I knew exactly what the dream was trying to tell me, I had been in denial for so long that I wasn't going into therapy prepared to accept the label as an incest survivor. Rena had her work cut out for her.

My sexual abuse secret had been dormant my entire life until this point, due in part that I had not met with any intuitive therapist who had detected abuse. After I had my first daughter in 2009, I went to a couple's therapist with my second husband, and she didn't detect the abuse either. It was buried deep, and I was a master of disguise. She assumed my intimacy issues with my ex were because we had drained our "love banks." She had us do exercises, such as sharing what we loved about each other. It's no wonder it didn't stick. Then I tried a male analyst, but he was useless. I would lie on the couch and talk, and he never said a word. But the dark secret of abuse was raging under my skin.

I knew I was slowly going crazy in my mind, but I didn't know why. Abuse denial is insidious. Unfortunately, therapy without revealing the abuse was like trying to bail water out of a rapidly sinking boat. If you have been to therapy and the abuse was not revealed, you are not alone. When the abuse does come to the surface, I recommend you see someone right away to be in your corner. If the expense of therapy worries you, look into finding a therapist who is covered by your insurance. There are also many therapists who take payment on a sliding scale, so don't be afraid to ask if you need some financial help. You deserve to heal and for someone with a degree on their wall to give you their undivided attention. Your healing is paramount so you can feel sane and healthy inside.

UNEARTHING

One of the greatest epiphanies I had in therapy was when I realized I had been seeking men's approval since the seventh grade when I felt pressure to look pretty at the dances. I always had a boyfriend, and we would hang out on the weekends. These young men would bring me comfort. I would stay at their houses and immerse myself in them. It was a pattern I had followed throughout my life, and part of it was black-and-white thinking, which ironically made me feel restricted, depressed, and panicked. I thought I had a "sex problem." My best thinking was, *Let's fix that.* I sought relief from the pattern of using my body as my best asset.

But one of the biggest revelations came to me in 2021 when I realized that a man I had a brief relationship with prior to sobriety and the abuse dream had date-raped me. Denial was still capable of rearing its ugly head.

It was 2011, and I was forty-one at the time. A friend referred me to a male therapist who specialized in sexual addictions. After our introductory session, the therapist looked at my ass as I walked out of the room, and I knew right then he wasn't going to help me come to terms with a "sex problem."

Although in a dysfunctional way, the ass-checking therapist became a part of my recovery journey. He asked me out a few days after our first meeting. Because my only real criterion for dating men at that time was their desire for me, I said yes. My disconnect from my feelings made me dangerously naive. I'd been married most of my adult life, so dating hadn't been an agenda. The therapist had money from his business ventures and wanted to spend it on me . . . while we got dirty. Sounds like solid boyfriend material, right? Flashback to my dad buying dinners and throwing one-hundred-dollar bills my way when I was in college. Abuse payoff. So I was just acting that out with this guy. Rather than seeking professional therapy, I decided I could "work out" my sexual issues by having "good sex." It never dawned on me that I sat in a room with this man and told him everything about my sexual proclivities and weaknesses, or that it was morally unethical for him to ask me out when I had interviewed him to be my therapist. He knew my secrets. I had no self-worth or awareness, so we began a relationship that involved a considerable amount of screwing, and he bought me a coffee maker, UGG boots, and a Kindle.

We dated for four months. I thought we were intimate, but I now realize it was a sexually misogynistic relationship. I was vulnerable after feeling sex-deprived from the last few years of my second marriage, so I thought this was my voyeur time. In fact, because he threw around money, I thought he was being nice to me because I was in a low place as a single mother. I didn't realize how low my bar was for men. I wanted to be loved. I believed he was the best I could accept at a time when I was on the verge of a breakthrough. He also took me to a few AA meetings, which planted a seed for my future sobriety.

But after some time, his belittling behaviors irritated me. I broke up with him and moved on. I had never broken it off with someone in four months' time, let alone someone who had instilled in me the notion that I didn't deserve to be in a loving relationship. It was so blatant, and the timing most definitely tipped the scales.

It wasn't until eight years later when I realized he had date-raped me. It happened on our second date. I had met him at his house during lunchtime to go for a walk. He was on a business call when I arrived, so I sat on the couch. He got off the call, and the next thing I knew, he was inside of me. I don't think I uttered a word. Afterward, we took our walk.

I ran into him several times after we split up. My eyes were slowly opening wider to what I had allowed myself to succumb to because I was no longer in denial. It was as if I was on a path to gradually learning what the therapist had done to me and facing it when I was ready. It would have been too much for me to face a date rape in the fundamental first few years of recovery from the childhood abuse.

When I finally unearthed what the therapist had done, I had so much rage and anger and emotion. I cried in my car. Then I chose to give it to God and let it go. As I worked on developing a new relationship with my inner self, I had to trust that there was another layer to this that would reveal itself. The anger indicated that fact. I could also sense the panic that came with this unearthing. I was honestly terrified of the therapist, just as I had been terrified of how my dad abused me on many levels.

Looking back, I realize I was in a state of shock when he date raped me. That's how dangerous it can be to avoid facing your truth. That was how little I valued my body and what could be done to it. I didn't say "no," so it wasn't technically a rape, and it appeared consensual, but in hindsight, the therapist did not ask for my permission. He just took what he wanted and silenced me.

I found solace in knowing why I had seen him that many times after that horrible day. God wanted me to see what I no longer was willing to accept and to now take my own protection firmly in my hands.

Years later, near the publication of this book, I bravely contacted the therapist to tell him my truth. I had no expectations. In fact, I expected him to deny it, which was exactly what he did. He told me I was going through a "challenging time." I told him I was, in fact, doing very well, but the time had come to speak my truth. What I didn't say was that I had justified or minimized the truth because I spent years in silence. I wasn't ready to boldly say, without fear of retribution, "What you did was wrong. Now you should talk to God about it." I won't ever know if our conversation had an impact on him. What I am most proud of is my willingness to recognize that I was still allowing abuse until I faced the denial.

There may be more to your story as you unravel your childhood abuse, depending how long you were in denial. Do not be surprised by what is revealed or blame yourself. Just lovingly keep tilling the soil and you will eventually reach the end of these incidents and traumas. Then you can focus on all the amazing new memories you get to make.

SEX ABUSE THERAPY

I was at rock bottom by the time I met with Rena, my sexual abuse therapist, in 2013. I had had the dream six months before, and despite having faced the abuse, I was still in some sort of denial. I wanted to be prepared to talk about all of my feelings before my first therapy session with Rena, so I did what I knew best: I wrote my ass off. This was the real deal: sexual abuse therapy after a lifetime of denial. It felt a little daunting. I wanted to have it all figured out *before* going to therapy so there would be no surprises. I battled with the voices in my head that told me I was being dramatic. *Maybe it's not as bad as you think. Do you really need to be so committed to this "concept?"* Suddenly, my entire life of fighting the dark secret of incest felt like an annoying itch. I discovered that my writing was trying to minimize the issue. *Well, now that you know about the abuse, is there more to discover?* The words on the page were taunting me. I believe I did this to protect myself from disappointment with the therapist if she turned out to be like the others. It's almost as if I didn't want her to see the real me. I thought she wouldn't believe me even if I told her.

The first day I went to therapy, I was split in two. On one hand, I was so unbelievably relieved I had finally come to the conclusion that I had been abused, but I also felt incredibly silly. I felt as if I had made up this ailment of denial because I had run out of excuses for why my life was derailed and erratic. On the day I staggered into that first therapy session—broken and beaten down by an angry life of substance abuse, sexual manipulation with men, and a lack of sexual self-care for myself—I knew I couldn't go on living my life this way. Change was on the horizon, and the dream was staring me down.

For most of 2013, when my kids went to their dad's house, I spent many afternoons in my bed, clutching my journal, writing, and weeping. Even if I was depressed, I would write about what it felt like to be "sick." My healing would symbolically take place under the covers, reversing the meaning from where the abuse occurred. I was taking ownership of the bed as my own place of personal sanctity and safety. Some days, I just hid when the world felt too vast and large.

My relationship with Rena would be like none other I had ever had. It didn't take long for the floodgates to open after I realized she wasn't going to doubt me. Splinters of memories of drives in the dark, hushed words, quiet visits, pleasure, confusion, desire, torment, and anger poured out of me. The feelings came fast and hard, all from the seven-year-old me.

Rena was never judgmental about what I said, or how hard I cried, or when I choked, gagged, turned red in the face, or went into catatonia. When she gave her opinion, she often accepted my resistance. She spent the first six months of our sessions listening to me sob and vent in disbelief and terror. I would leave her office so despondent. I would be on the street in Santa Monica on a sunny Tuesday afternoon and feel like a warped, lost alien. The world was a weapon. There was no safe space. During therapy, I gradually gained my footing and began to leave her office feeling as if I had gained something rather than being ground down like glass.

In my sessions, I confessed my anger at my mother, expressing how much it sucked that she didn't protect or love me enough as a kid. She worked hard, and when she was home, she was distant and frustrated in her marriage. She didn't have the bandwidth to understand what was going on in her daughter's bed when I needed her to make it stop. She also never tried to really understand who I was as a young woman. Rena showed me what it was like to have a woman listen to you, be trustworthy, and be present.

THE SECOND DREAM

One of my happier childhood memories was at a Bahá'í family camp. I befriended a towheaded blonde boy one summer, and I still remember feeling complete euphoria as I ran around the grassy fields and knolls with him. The innocence and the balance of our youth. A few months into therapy, I had another dream. I was seven or eight years old, and my dad was picking me up at the Bahá'í retreat in an old 1960s sedan. He was wearing a trench coat, and I knew I didn't want to get into the car with him. I had to say goodbye to the blonde boy I had met on the retreat—my first innocent crush. I had a sinking, hideous feeling about getting into the car with my dad. I was leaving what was safe and innocent and heading into the darkness. I didn't want to go back to the male world that was old and mature and sexual and scary. I wanted to stay with the young boy.

For years after, I still couldn't recall the name of the camp. I kept praying for it to come to me. One day, the name appeared in my memory: Green Acres, and it was located in Maine. I looked it up online, and tears streamed down my face when I saw a picture of the place. I emailed the enrollment director and asked if they had a roster of the kids who were there in 1976 or 1977. They didn't, but they told me about some alumni groups. I wasn't able to find that boy, but it was a key memory in starting the process of realizing what had been taken from me through abuse when I was a small child.

Part of the monkey wrench in my therapeutic process was my lack of memory. The dreams were few and far between, as were the flashbacks. Not only did my ten-year-old self have to deal with a decade of abuse, but there was an absence when the abuse stopped. I was left with a paralyzing sense that an epic part of my upbringing had ended abruptly. If someone loves you in a certain way and then cuts it off, the secret dies in the silence and loneliness. I don't remember the day when the abuse ended, but the age of ten stands out for me. I don't question it. I have to trust what I feel inside, and what the dreams reveal to me.

In therapy, there were waves of remembering the essence of abuse, mostly the touching, but the memories were never graphic or specific. They may be buried down there. It is possible I had disassociated from my body so well that recalling it now, forty years later, is too difficult.

DON'T LEAVE BEFORE THE MIRACLE

For several years, I worked with Rena every week. We talked about trust issues and coping mechanisms for when the truth paralyzed me. We talked about getting clear on what I wanted in a partner, or how to explore sexuality after learning I had a history of abuse. I soon found myself attending sessions where I was actually bored and thought, *Maybe I don't need therapy anymore. I am wasting my time and money. I have peaked in my revelations.* Translation: a colossal breakthrough was right around the corner.

They say in recovery, "Don't leave before the miracle happens." I stayed in therapy for longer than I wanted to because I had a hunch there was more to remember, to walk through. Some days I wanted to quit. *Enough suffering!* I would think. Our old self wants to keep protecting us because it doesn't think we can handle the truth. It creates exit strategies for us because we had none when we were abused. We couldn't leave and had to stay until it was over, so we used our brain to exit the situation. As adults, we need to tell the inner-child brain that we have a handle on the situation and can now go deeper. Make the magic. Find the solutions. Step into a life that is bigger, vaster, and more abundant than we could ever imagine.

I went into therapy one day and expressed my fear of not being able to prove my worth through sex with men. I had put a pause on dating for a few months and was spending more time on myself. Rena held space for me as I rambled on about my emptiness and loneliness. Then a great wave of emotion washed over me. A monsoon of tears poured from my eyes and down my face.

"I don't want to be in this body anymore," I sobbed uncontrollably. "It's ravaged and abused and torn, and it doesn't fit to where my mind is growing and going."

I was outgrowing my body in its old form as I made a new mind-body connection with myself in recovery, and I didn't know how to feel. All I wanted to do was reject the old vessel. I didn't believe it could carry the recovered me inside an old shell. I left that session feeling gutted but also so happy that I had been honest about how beaten down my body felt. I didn't believe my body had the potential to rejuvenate and grow. But I also realized I didn't need a man to prove my worth by giving my body away, and I didn't need to loathe my body anymore. I would not have had this profound conversation with my therapist if I had left my therapy commitment when my mind told me to cut and run.

I talk later in this book about listening and honoring your body. You want to stay connected to your current body state as you work through the cognitive aspects of your trauma. You want to look compassionately at the whole you who needs to heal. Your body has been through so much and gotten you here to get better. Your legs have carried you throughout the years. Your feet have walked miles. Your arms and hands have played an instrument or hugged a loved one. Your smile has brightened someone's day.

Look at your body. Witness yourself taking ownership of your body as your own. Your body transports you to where you want to be in your life. You get to have a new relationship with your body while you are working out the mental piece in therapy.

Here are a few questions to help you align your mind-body connection:

- Who are you in your body? How do you feel about your

shoulders, arms, and ribs? Touch them. Do they feel sexy and part of your beautiful body?

- What can you do to soothe your face? We carry a lot of tension in our face. You could try tapping it, rubbing the muscles of your jaw, or using a jade roller.

- How are your feet? Do you like your feet? Can you pamper them?

YOU NEED SUPPORT TO HEAL

As you walk down the road of abuse recovery, you will need a lot of support in your community. People who have been abused should not spend too much time alone or in silence. While you don't have to tell your entire story to everyone you meet, you can lean on sponsors and fellows in twelve-step programs, business coaches, life coaches, branding coaches, networking groups, listening partnerships, dates, and friends. If you stay curious about how you are healing, your support system will fill in the gaps of your life that are still empty in a loving way. No, we don't need to dump our stuff on everyone, but living life, sharing, and commiserating is part of the healthy human condition. We want to get into the "normal" part of life. Your recovery can bring you to the truth of your gifts in this world. You might be surprised to unearth who you are.

I questioned my therapist many times in my therapeutic process. *Maybe Rena isn't deep enough. Do we chat about my kids too much in our sessions? I think she should do more inner-child work. I should be sobbing and freaking out every time I go in, not just once a month.* I was honest with her about my concerns. I had to be. In my recovery, I was practicing how to use my voice to get what I wanted and needed.

I eventually stopped going to therapy when I was fully neutral with the decision that I was complete. I no longer felt terrorized by my abuse memories, and I could identify the feelings associated with abuse trauma when they arose. I was tired of rehashing the same thought pattern over and over. I was ready to apply my findings to life. Rena questioned whether I was ready, but standing my ground boosted my confidence and gave me back my power. It was a choice, and I made it clean. I had options in life. If I chose not to go to therapy for a while and then needed to go back, I knew where to find her. She would be there waiting for me with open arms. I know if I do go back, it will be for a new layer, and I will approach the discovery with curiosity and not fear. If you are at a point in therapy where you feel confident enough to know you are done, it should feel effortless. Even if you leave therapy before you are ready, you can make a clear choice to go back. Therapy is for you and on your terms.

Therapists are like a tugboat as you head out in the vast sea of life. I needed a weekly guidepost until I could make sense of my new life on my own, so continuing therapy through new experiences of visibility and change was a smart decision for me. Not everyone wants to talk to a therapist, and that is okay too. There are many other methods and therapies for healing trauma, such as eye movement desensitization and reprocessing (EMDR), cognitive processing therapy (CPT), and cognitive behavioral therapy (CBT). Everyone's healing journey is different. You just have to find what works for you.

THOUGHT-PROVOKING QUESTIONS

Have you started therapy of some kind for your abuse? What were your feelings and emotions in the first session? If you haven't started therapy, why?

What therapists have come and gone in your life? Can you see where they might have been either right or wrong for you? If you are looking for a therapist, write down what you want to share with them. Interview them. This is a vital partnership for recovery.

Do you have fanciful and free memories of your childhood when you were safe from the abuse?

Do you remember how you felt when the abuse ended? I am aware this may be impossible for some people to remember. I don't recall the day itself, but when I lean into the page, I can recall the free-falling state. See where the moment takes you.

Have you ever felt like nothing was happening in therapy and then there was a big breakthrough? Document those sessions so you can have more faith in therapy's natural course.

Chapter 7

TELLING OTHERS

The timing of when and how to tell someone about your abuse can feel complicated and loaded. People you tell will range from friends and family, to telling your story to an audience on a public platform. You may even confront your abuser if it is safe. As a survivor, you will intuitively know when the time is right to tell others. Be gentle with yourself if you share your story before you are ready, or if you blurt it out to someone who hasn't been vetted as a confidant. Having a voice is the most important part of healing. The people who may not have been the best choices to share your story with will eventually forget. You are the one who holds the deep truth that needs to get out.

Sharing my story was a rocky but freeing journey for me, and it took a few years for me to be candid about it in appropriate circles. Having the first conversations with trusted family members can pave the path for harder conversations, such as with a parent. I do not have experience confronting my abuser. My dad was long dead by the time I came out of denial. Confronting is a completely different category than telling. Only you know how to show up for that conversation, but I urge you to still do the steps and the outreach I discuss in this chapter, and then see what comes from there. Always remember that this is for you to heal, not get revenge.

We can be wounded again by other people's despair at our secret, so make sure you know when to end the conversation. A good time to end the conversation is when you feel angry or their reaction to your story is lacking compassion. Tap into how you feel in your body during the conversation and wrap it up before you become overwhelmed. This is your story, and you can take ownership of how and when you tell it.

SHARING YOUR STORY

When you tell your family about your abuse, it can dismantle the fabric of their history. They may not like this new version of the past and can react in a way that feels frustrating, which is why you need to lean on other supporters. Telling your story can also bring on a wave of shame. The *victim* role can come up—the "why me?" We are upset that sexual abuse is even part of our story. If you are still in a state of raw emotions when you discuss your abuse, it is best to have your truths validated first in a therapy office, support group, or twelve-step program. Then you can have a bit more detachment when you are ready to tell others.

Some family members will be saddened by the news. Regardless of how others react, you must remember that sharing your truth is one of the most difficult but brave openings of self. You are orchestrating a voice you did not have when you couldn't say no to the abuse. When you finally decide to tell someone, know that you are on the path to breaking the silence, to fading a dark sense of futility, and cracking open the door of a fresh beginning.

The following sections offer advice on how to reveal your sexual abuse story to family members, other survivors, and even the people you are dating.

TELLING A SIBLING

I told my sister before I told my mom. My only sibling is eight years younger than me, and we had been estranged for over a decade. I struggled to understand why she didn't want a relationship with me and disliked me so much, but I hoped revealing my history of abuse with our dad could bring healing to us and our own fraught history.

When my sister was born, I was angry. On the surface, it might have appeared to my mom that I was just a horrible older sister. My mom was horrified by my rage when I found my sister in my room ransacking my precious vinyl collection. "How could you be so angry?" my mom had said to me. I was routinely punished for acting out. Many decades later, when I was in a relationship with my husband and the father of my children, he would ask me, "Why are you so angry?" I did not know why I was so angry until I faced the abuse. The childhood anger and the secrets affected how I could be honest about what and who I wanted in my life. Instead, I attracted people who blindly poked the finger at me. I also needed to start talking and telling my story, and my family of origin appeared to be key. I had no idea the well would be so dry.

I didn't feel comfortable bombarding my sister with my story over the phone, so I texted her to ask if we could talk. I was at home when I called, and I was not nervous. In fact, I was strangely calm. I had made myself devoid of emotion, which was a safe space for me with people I didn't trust or know. She had been untrustworthy in her abandonment of me as a sister, and I did not want to tap into that pain on the call.

"I am facing the fact that I was sexually abused by our dad for a long time," I said, then waited for her response as I held my breath. It was not what I expected.

"That explains everything," she said.

That was exactly what my ex-husband had said when I called him after the dream. I was noticing a pattern with the people from my past.

She shared that she was no longer interested in having dark conversations in her life. She wanted to keep things light and polite. I felt ashamed that I had told her, as if I was in some way propagating the abuse, but I knew in my heart that wasn't the case. I needed people in my family of origin to know. If they hated me for it, that was on them. I pray that one day, with the passage of time and healing, my sister and I will come together again and talk now that I am no longer in denial, but I had to give that possibility to God.

CONFESSING IN DATING

We also carry the "I am damaged" card, which is disguised under the ruse of "open honesty." This is where we start down the slippery slope of telling people so we can trauma-bond. When I first found out about the abuse, I told the men I was dating right away. Like a warning beacon to them: *Watch out for this one because she is a survivor and pissed as fuck.* I still thought that angry little girl was inside of me.

When I used to tell men early in the relationship, I found myself playing the role of seducer to dominate the scared, vulnerable feelings I felt as a survivor in the dating world. I would morph into a performance model. *I can give a mean lap dance! I am so sexually fascinating and free!* Yet, this was all false bravado from an unhealed woman who needed validation by what she had been shown as love: sexuality. I am not implying that your sexual freedom and adventure with your partner indicates that you are acting out on trauma. The key is to know what is driving this desire to be "seen in your sexual parts," whether it is related to revealing your past or stamping down the pain of over-sexualization.

I was in a three-month relationship when I dropped the abuse bomb over eggs at breakfast. It landed so awkwardly and poorly because I was still telling the men about it as if it were something they should know about me (for example, "I am broken."). I knew of this person's inability to hold emotional space for me, but I persisted for three months, and despite the warning signs that the relationship wasn't going to work out, I still felt compelled to tell my story.

I later learned how to soothe my inner child, who had been sexualized way too young. Then, as I got to a healthier place in my healing, even if I went on three or four dates with a man, I did not tell them about the abuse. I had to decide whether they were worthy of me before I let them into my life and shared my personal history. I reached a point where I couldn't fathom dating someone and then telling them I was an incest survivor. *I will never know how to have this conversation again in a healthy way,* I would think. Of course, this is not true. When I felt the secret was interfering with my ability to open up in other ways in the relationship, I told them the truth about my past.

While we choose partners to help us heal parts of ourselves, they are not dumping grounds for our untreated wounds. We can practice maturity in timing versus the urgent desire to vomit a truth like an injured, fractured little child. My emotional support circle had widened, giving me the freedom to talk about the abuse and how it affected my daily well-being without having to share it with the men I was dating. Male or female friends and recovery circles can be a safe place to land.

I also had spirituality and prayer, having returned after so long to form a relationship with a loving and nonjudgmental God. I could talk to God before dates. I am naturally impatient, so five dates felt like a lifetime, and I was eager to share my story. But I had to keep an eye on the frightened, nervous feeling that I was using the abuse to create some kind of intimacy bond with the person. *I told you my secret, now love me.* Underneath it all was a self-fulfilling prophecy that they would see me as damaged regardless, so I reasoned that I might as well get it over with.

If you don't want to tell every person you're dating about your abuse, I suggest creating a list of other subjects to discuss before the date and sticking to them. Remind yourself that your abuse was real, that your memories are not a lie, and that you now get to have a full life where you can explore how to rewire your adult life with love. Everyone you go on a date with is dealing with something, and we get a chance to show up with imperfection, but we also don't have to lay all of our past shame on the table over the appetizer.

SHARING WITH OTHER SURVIVORS

God puts people in our path who have already dealt with the abuse and can serve as conduits for our healing. At the end of 2014, I was working on a television project with a confident, beautiful woman, a mother of two who had been married to a doting man for twenty years. When the kids were at school, the writing sessions took place at her house, and she always had some kind of yummy home-baked dish prepared, such as enchiladas or quinoa casserole. Because I was surrounded by the comforts of home, I felt open and intimate in this friendship. We would talk about our personal lives, which is typical in writing relationships. One day, I told her that my father had sexually abused me.

"I was abused too," she said without missing a beat.

I stared at her in shock. "Really?"

She nodded. "Yup. By multiple perpetrators when I was younger."

This woman had everything. She was a model, a mother, and a businesswoman. It made me realize how many women out there had been abused but didn't talk about it. This woman was strong. She didn't take crap from anyone.

"Did you tell your mom?" I asked.

"Sure," she said. "But she didn't really have a reaction."

"When did you tell her?" I asked, on the edge of my seat.

"In my early twenties. I moved on from my mother's ambivalence," she said.

"I don't know when it's a good time to tell my mom," I said, feeling bad that I had wasted my entire life harboring my secret.

"You'll know when you are ready because it will be easy."

TELLING A PARENT

I debated whether my mom knew about the abuse, or if she would be ambivalent or deny it. What would I do if she said that she didn't know about the abuse? Would I accept it, or did I truly believe a mother would not know incest was happening in her own home? I thought about my daughters, and while I didn't live with a husband, their dad was safe. I was cognizant of my daughters' lives and their moods. I noticed a shift or change. Was I really such a master of disguise when it came to my childhood abuse? Every time I considered telling my mom about my abuse, I had to wait until the hot feeling in my face passed because I loathed her so much for not protecting me. I didn't approach her until I was in a place of neutrality. I wrote about the abuse, and it was empowering to document the unraveling of my old self and the reconstruction of my new life without attacking anyone. I wanted my story to be clear for other people who were still suffering, so I had to follow the timeline of when the words would tell me my next action. They did.

I remember the afternoon when I was ready. It was 2014, and I was sitting in a coffee shop on the west side of Los Angeles when the voice hit me like a thunderbolt: *You have to write your mom the email right now.* It had been six months since I had told my sister, who I assumed never said anything to our mother even though they talked.

The email just flowed out of me. My heart was pounding out

of my chest like a small, scared child when I hit Send. Then I emailed my friend.

"I sent it."

She immediately sent me an email back: "Now go live and make what you want from life a reality!"

I left the coffee shop and sobbed in my car. My friend was right. It was time to be set free, and this was just the beginning.

My mom's reaction to the email was one of sympathy. She wanted to talk on the phone. She said she had never known about the abuse, and she was so sorry. My feelings were split between empathy and blame. How could a wife not know her spouse was sexually abusing their daughter for a decade? As a young mother, she was very controlling and operated from a place of rigor and perfectionism. It seemed so unfathomable that she never suspected anything.

When I got on the phone with my mom, the first thing she said was, "I am so sorry. I had no idea."

I could tell she was struggling with the fact that her entire past, her own marriage, was disintegrating all around her. She was pushing through to honor my pain and the experience we were having about me and my recovery. After we talked for a half hour or so, she said, "Now you can have your power back."

I hated her for it as much as I loved her for it. Honestly, I was just grateful she didn't deny it. I was afraid she would demand facts. It didn't really matter what she said or how she reacted because this was for me, not for her. When she cried, there was no defensive position I could take. I just sat in the space and let her have her feelings.

The cloak of denial weighed heavily on her shoulders as it had on mine. For decades, we shared that burden in silence.

"I am not blaming you," I said to her. If I wanted to continue to have a relationship with my mom, then I couldn't attack her.

"I know," she said.

"So . . ." I said. "What else is going on?" I felt the need to progress the conversation into some kind of mundane normalcy. That was the people pleaser in me. I still didn't know how to use my voice to say, "I need to get off the phone and not act like this was just a normal catch-up call." So I let her tell me about her condo renovation for a few minutes before we got off the phone.

A few days later, I was on the verge of a complete nervous breakdown. I was sitting in my car, thinking, *I can't do this. I can't handle all that is opening inside of me.* I did not have the capacity to take on this truth, the lies, the loss of childhood, and the lack of protection I was given. I wanted to fill my body with an entire bottle of wine and take lots of Valium. But I was nine months sober at that time and determined to make it through one year without any drugs or alcohol. What I truly needed was a soft blanket and pillow, and for someone to make me food and hold me, and to let me sleep and cry through the pain in a safe place. Besides, I hate Valium.

I've learned that strong support systems of women survivors (or other ways you may identify, whether that is male, nonbinary, LGBTQ+, etc.) provide a safe space to share your vulnerability, doubts, confusion, and desperation. They are best equipped to hold you as your secret seeps out into the many corners of your life. Meeting the new you can be painful, especially when none of the stages of processing the abuse appear to lead to happiness. They do. I am a testament to that truth.

I wish I had allowed myself to be angrier after I told my mother about the abuse. I had become too swayed by peace, love, and harmony and had bypassed my true feelings. I had wanted to be a good daughter and visit her, and to provide her access to my children. I get crazy in my head if I think about how my mom could not know. Was she so deep asleep that she didn't hear my dad leaving their bed and go down the hall to my room? Where was she every night when he stroked my body parts to sleep? I could ponder so many variations of that story until the cows come home, but that is in the past. While I don't need to close the door on it, I also don't need to waste away the present obsessing over facts I will never know.

I kept the relationship with my mother going for many years after our conversation. I tried to love her and give her the space to heal. Then, one day, we had a disagreement over the phone about religion. Because of the COVID-19 pandemic, I had not seen her in over a year. Like many others, I did a lot of deep soul searching during the pandemic to find more self-love and reflection. I took several soul-retrieval journeys with the Shaman community, and I truly felt that I was an outsider in my history and in my childhood. Everyone in the legacy of abuse was dead except for my mom and sister. All of my mom's siblings, both sets of grandparents, my dad the abuser . . . all gone. That existence was something like a different reality, and I could choose to let it go. I had learned from it. So when my mother and I had a disagreement about my going to church, she said, "Stop acting like a child . . . fuck you," and hung up on me. I didn't call her back. I don't chase people who swear at me and cut me off. There are people in my life who reflect back to me the best versions of myself, not the old, broken parts. My mother and I went into a two-year period of silence. It was a long time coming. Over the course of my life, I had the time to heal my disappointment in the relationship with my mother. I felt abandoned, not financially supported, and that she was there just for the sake of convenience. As survivors, we don't need to sign up for a relationship with anyone who treats us with any kind of abuse, even if they are our parents.

I finally called her to break the silence, and the conversation went very poorly. We do not see each other in the best light, but that is okay. I am close to other survivors who have also put their relationship with their parents to rest. Just for today, I feel peace about it. Miracles can happen, and we may heal our relationship one day.

In order to preserve the rest of my life as a place of wholeness within me, I had to completely step out of that past paradigm. If you think that sounds too harsh, look at how you are letting the people who were involved with your abuse history off the hook. We all have our own forgiveness processes, and the truth is that you can forgive, but who is forcing you to engage? Sometimes telling your story opens the door to a reality you don't want to embrace, but at least it's of your own making.

TELLING YOUR ABUSE STORY: A PROCESS

I suffered with doubt many times in recovery. I even almost gave up writing this book because I felt guilty about publicly calling out my dead dad. I called my AA sponsor with tears in my eyes.

"I don't know if I can finish this book. What if I am wrong?" I cried.

Luckily, she had been with me the entire time as a witness to all of my breakdowns and breakthroughs.

"Oh honey," she said to me. "It so happened. No way it didn't."

I was so glad to have her in my court. I continued writing the book.

I can give you hope that your history as a sexual abuse survivor will one day help others 95 percent of the time if you have the right mindset and belief system. And when that 5 percent tries to make you put up a wall or protect the little girl or boy in the bed, you have enough awareness to know it'll be okay. It's done. Nobody is going to sexually abuse you again.

There are forums dedicated to survivors of sexual abuse. Help for Adult Victims of Child Abuse (HAVOCA) has a large international forum online. "Telling others about your abuse is a difficult but courageous task. It can be as much empowering to you as it seems frightening. Best of all, telling a safe person allows you to get your experience out into the open and not still bottled up inside of you. Silence is a dangerous thing; it is a stumbling block in the healing process. With courage and hard work, you too can remove all the stumbling blocks on the path of healing and reclaim your life."[5]

The following sections will walk you through the process of sharing your abuse story. How you share your story, and with whom, is important depending on your style of communication and comfort level. You may not get the reaction you hoped for, so you can prepare for some disappointment. I wish someone had broken this down for me when I was first coming out of denial. I hope it makes your journey a little less haphazard.

Understand Your Story

As discussed in chapter 2, understanding your own story is an important first step in your abuse recovery. If you have been in denial, chances are that many of the details are a blur. In order to feel confident and ready to open up about your story, it is suggested to write it down. We must first tackle our own mind games that may diminish or justify the abuse. You will want to turn off doubt before telling someone who may doubt you.

Your story can be written in a notebook or on a computer. The goal of this exercise is for you to write down your story *for you*. Here are some questions to think about:

[5] "Telling Our Family, Friends, and Acquaintances About Our Abuse," HAVOCA, accessed August 21, 2022, https://www.havoca.org/first-step/telling-others/.

- What are some of your unanswered questions about your abuse?

- Who knew about the abuse?

- Why didn't anyone say something or report your abuse if they were aware of it?

- What were they unaware of, and why were they unaware of it? Be as specific as possible.

This list is not to work you up into a frothy point of accusation, anger, and contention, but to have clarity and purpose when you do start to make inquiries.

Make a List

After you have finished writing down the details of your abuse, the second step is to choose someone to tell your story to. Here are a few considerations when you are telling someone about your abuse:

- Make a list of the people you want to tell. Ask yourself why you want to tell these people. I told one of my cousins because he was like a brother to me, but I didn't tell my other two cousins. I also wanted to see if he remembered anything because my memory was so spotty. I told my best friend because I wanted to be honest and open about my bad days as I worked through my recovery.

- After you've made the list, choose someone you trust to tell first. It could be a friend, family member, or another survivor who has identified themselves at a recovery meeting, church, or in a social group. You want compassion and kindness on the first telling. Be watchful of sharing with anyone who gossips or is connected to you professionally. People can exploit what they may perceive as a weakness against you. I know it sounds harsh, but some people do not see survival as a strength.

Reach Out and Share Your Story

- After you have decided who to tell, send them a short email or text. Don't tell them why you are reaching out to them just yet. Simply say something like, "Hi, I would like to grab a few moments of your time on the phone. When would be the best time to chat?" If they ask questions about the nature of the call, tell them that you would prefer to speak with them over the phone or in person. Don't get drawn into a back-and-forth text or email exchange, as this will affect your healing. Remember, this person does not know your story. Stay firm and kind. If they insist on knowing before you can talk or meet, you may want to consider if they are in the right space for you to do this powerful energetic work.

- When you are ready to share your story, you can begin by saying, "This may be difficult to hear, but because you are my family, or my close friend, I want you to know I was abused. I am working through this truth after a long denial, and part of my healing is for the people I know and love to be a part of my healing." They may ask questions or just be shocked. You should take your emotional temperature during your reveal. You may be triggered if you reveal too many details, so be mindful of your mental state.

Aftermath

After you tell someone your story, do not overthink every word of the conversation. Your self-esteem can be very low in sexual abuse recovery, so you could be prone to beating yourself up. Don't do it. Evaluate your thoughts and ask yourself these questions:

- Am I satisfied with their response?

- What more has been revealed?

- What can I learn from this conversation to improve my future storytelling?

Let your new set of questions help you clarify whether telling your story got the benefits and outcomes you hoped for. I can't stress this enough: telling your story is for your own healing from the denial. The other person's reaction or denial is not as relevant as you might think. Every time you use your once-silenced voice, you are gaining momentum and strength.

Telling others is not a race. Once you start sharing your story, you will soon be open to tell everyone. While some of the people on my list came later down the road, each person I told gave me the courage to be there for another survivor. I gained a sense of triumph in facing my abuse. There is no way to heal from sexual abuse if you keep it bottled up inside, and I wanted to share that understanding with others who were still scared.

The truth is that no matter who we tell about the abuse, the most important story we get to rewrite in our recovery from sexual abuse denial is the one we tell ourselves.

THOUGHT-PROVOKING QUESTIONS

Do you believe you have a responsibility to tell your partners that you had been abused? Examine whether you believe you are bringing a stigma against you into your romantic life.

What would you gain by holding on to the truth that you were abused? Can you punch holes in some of those false protections?

Can you be okay with not talking to certain family members or people in your life who you believe may have been aware of the abuse but did nothing about it?

Chapter 8

TAKING BACK YOUR BODY

When you have been abused, you don't know how to take care of yourself. Self-abuse can occur when you fail to get routine checkups or ignore ailments or conditions that could be treated with proper medical care. You may also avoid asking medical professionals questions because you're afraid they'll think you're crazy or a hypochondriac. This results in the opposite extreme where you are neglecting yourself.

Because you have been denying the sexual abuse for so long, you have been entrapped and are holding your secret inside. This solo effort of self-preservation, even if it's subconscious, signals to your physiology that you are on your own. You may believe you have to solve your own health problems and can't ask anyone for help. You have cut yourself off from a whole world of solutions. Then self-hate comes into play. *I don't deserve to be better.* You don't believe your body has any value or worth.

The buried secrets and denial are embedded deep within the very fabric of your cells and DNA. This has an effect on how you approach your body and care for it. Since I did not tell anyone what my perpetrator was doing to my body, either out of fear or loyalty, a belief was created that it wasn't real or I had made it up in my head. This type of thinking results in a warped perception in all areas of your adult life. *Did that happen or not? Maybe I shouldn't say anything because people will think I am an alarmist.* At a young age, I lost that intuitive validation of what is healthy to express for my own safety, security, and happiness. So when I was an adult, I didn't want to be dramatic about my body ailments or tell anyone, and I used wishful thinking to try to will the problem away.

For a lifetime, I treated my body with the same energy it had when it was under the control of the abuser. My body was a foreign object to me. I had no connection to it, let alone any kind of mind-body-spirit connection. When I was in denial, my body oozed the darkness out of me, and I was clueless. As we heal emotionally, we start to track physical ailments that are connected to our repression of sexual abuse. Before recovery, I had no idea that my body was acting out repressed dark inner secrets. We just don't know what we are supposed to be listening to, so how can we listen?

You now have an opportunity to start listening to your body and reclaiming its knowledge that the abuser has taken from you. You were conditioned to say yes to others but not to tune into yourself. Your body was the vessel that carried your unshaped spirit, and it manifested disease and trauma to both protect and loathe itself. The body is a fascinating communicator for our mind. They are deeply interconnected. Louise Hay, self-help pioneer and author of *You Can Heal Your Body*, believed physical ailments and diseases can reveal unresolved trauma, anger, and resentment.[6] When we disassociate as survivors, we distance ourselves so severely from the beauty of our bodies.

I talk about how abuse affects eating and body image in chapter 17, but here I want to focus more about the disconnect, and how incredibly powerful the mind is at fabricating damage that confirms our brokenness.

---

[6] Louise Hay, *You Can Heal Your Life,* (New York: Hay House Publishing, 2008).

MY AILMENTS

I had a lifelong body ailment that went away as I got closer to facing the abuse, and then a condition emerged after I faced it. I tell my stories in depth so you can see where you relate. Our bodies can be mirrors to our emotional healing, and a body inventory can help you explore how your body has absorbed the stress of trauma. I am a firm believer in the mind-body connection, so when we look at our health issues in recovery, we can shift our perspective from what is being done to us, to what is happening in us, and take a more authoritative stand in our healing. When we no longer deny abuse, we can channel that awareness into championing our body's health and healing. At the end of this chapter, you will get a chance to write your own ailment inventory.

Herpes

When I was eighteen, I was diagnosed with herpes, a sexually transmitted disease (STD). I had accepted this diagnosis as truth and fact because the diagnosis subconsciously confirmed what I thought about myself: I am a dirty woman.

It was the summer of 1988 after my freshman year in college, and I was working on Cape Cod as a waitress with a best friend. We were wild, drunk, and free but I was not promiscuous. I had only one boyfriend prior, so my version of sleeping around paled in comparison to other young adults we hung out with on the Cape. I had a one-night stand without protection (my generation was terrible about using condoms), and I woke up with burning sores. I went straight to the emergency room. A tired-looking doctor examined me. Without a hint of emotion and a little disgust on his face, he told me I had herpes.

I was stunned. "That can't be possible," I said. *I'm not even a slut*, I thought.

Then it hit me. I would have this STD for the rest of my life.

"I'll give you a minute to process this, and I'll send in a nurse to discuss treatment," he said.

"Okay," I croaked. *Treatment?* I'd read about the Big H. There was no treatment. Herpes was uber contagious with no cure in sight, so I would have to tell everyone I slept with that I had herpes if I had an outbreak. I never considered how painful sex with an outbreak could be. There was no compassion for myself or anger about one of those dudes giving me herpes. It was confirmed: I was dirty and damaged.

I told my first husband about my affliction before we started getting physical. It was the honorable thing to do. "So, I think you are great, and we are clearly attracted to each other, but I need to tell you something. I have herpes."

In retrospect, it was a perfect setup for me to immediately expose how damaged and unlovable I was. I reasoned: *If you take me with this scar of imperfection, then it means you really care about me. Therefore, I'll take you no matter what, even if it means destroying you because I have worse secrets I won't face.*

Never once did I consider getting a second opinion from that Cape Cod doctor. Never once did I go for a blood test. The crazy part is that I had debilitating outbreaks for decades. I used the outbreaks to avoid having sex with my first and my second husbands. What was most astounding was that my outbreaks worsened when my dad came to town. I would tell him about them, and he'd be mildly sympathetic. On one visit, the sores hurt so much that I was limping. I tried the old-fashioned remedies. I would sit on the toilet and cry as I dabbed the sores with gauze pads soaked in witch hazel. Entire weekends were saddened by this curse. I drank gallons of raw cranberry juice and took lysine. Alcohol would exacerbate the symptoms, so I smoked pot to escape. My body was making sure the predator didn't lay a hand on me, so it gave me the fiercest fire of defense.

When my children were born, I even took special medication in case the herpes flared up from the stress because I was terrified of my kids being born blinded by the open sores. I was relieved when both babies were delivered via C-section.

When I divorced my second husband in 2012, I went to a new ob/gyn. I was immediately attracted to him, and I sensed his attraction to me as well. I should have left right then and there and found another gynecologist, but I didn't. Instead, I told him I wanted to get the status of the herpes in check because I wanted to start dating. I hadn't had an outbreak in over five years (my dad had been dead for six), and I had felt a sore down there.

The doctor examined the sore and said it wasn't herpes. "Aside from your original diagnosis in 1988, have you had a blood test to diagnose if you have herpes?" he asked.

I was baffled. A blood test? I was told I had herpes and had been living with it for the past two decades. Then I realized that I'd never given it to anyone. I was taking a birth control pill for most of my life, so I didn't use condoms with my husbands. The doctor took bloodwork.

The next day I got the news. I tested negative for herpes.

I was blown away. I sobbed in the examination room. Even the doctor was shocked. He couldn't understand why I had never gotten a second opinion. I had signed up for some bullshit branding at eighteen. That was part of my sexual abuse repression.

So I went right to my next best idea: I had a brief, torrid sexual affair with him. Of course I did! He was my angel! He had freed me with miraculous news, so he deserved my fresh and clean vagina! Herpes-free sex to celebrate! It didn't take much convincing to get him to oblige. All I had to do was agree to no longer be his patient. At that point, I didn't give a shit. I was laser focused on having herpes-free sex with someone for the first time in twenty-five years.

This was the beginning of my sexual low point and downward spiral. It was this bottom that contributed to me finally having the dream that forced me to face the sexual abuse. It was this bottom that showed me how erratically I had gone off course in my life.

I was not sexually timid in my marriages, but I was protected by the monogamy. Now that I was single and left to my own devices, I took pictures of myself in dressing rooms wearing lingerie. I made videos of me masturbating in restaurant bathrooms and sent them to him. When I got tired of him, I moved on to the next guy and repeated the same behavior. My abused inner soul was heading to a dark pit of despair. This sexual expression was not joyous or free. It was sad and lonely. I still didn't know how to cope with or celebrate the fact that my body was telling me something. I wasn't listening. I treated my body like some baggage I was carrying on my back. I didn't celebrate not having herpes with a day at the spa. My best idea was to get laid as much as possible.

Fortunately, this phase was brief. As much as I wanted to act out, there was a reason deep down I had been monogamous in two marriages for two decades. I was still looking for love. My sad, little girl self was convinced that she would never find love, so she resorted to using what she thought was her best assets to survive: her vagina and her sexuality.

When I started therapy for sexual abuse, I had clarity. The "Ghost Herpes," as I called it, was my body's reaction to the repressed sexual abuse. It may sound strange, but the Ghost Herpes were, in fact, real. The denial manifested in lesions on my vagina. I was in real pain and took medication for it. There are women who have false pregnancies, in which they exhibit signs and symptoms of being pregnant—tender breasts, a growing belly, missed periods—but they are not pregnant. Some of these women can even feel the "baby" move. This pseudopregnancy can be caused by trauma.[7]

When I was in relationships with men who had the potential for emotional intimacy (such as both of my husbands), the Ghost Herpes flared up to protect me by controlling what I could use: sex. I could say, "Oh, sorry, but I'm having an outbreak and can't be intimate with you. Stay away from me because I'm sick and damaged, and I am going to isolate and nurse my wounded self in the corner." So, on one hand, it kept a deepening of intimacy at bay, but it also protected me from promiscuity that could have turned into infidelity. Abuse survivors can become promiscuous. That wasn't my story. The debilitating sores hindered my sexual freedom even in my marriages and kept me in shame. When I received the diagnosis that it wasn't herpes, the outbreaks went away, and the stage was set for me to open my body and mind up to facing the memories of the abuse. In reflection, I am blown away by my body's capacity to create a protection mechanism on so many levels

Let me be perfectly clear: there is no shame associated with having herpes. The Centers for Disease Control and Prevention (CDC) estimates that there are approximately 572,000 new genital herpes (herpes simplex virus, type 2 (HSV-2) infections in the United States in a single year.[8] I know people who live with it shame-free, but I also know abuse survivors who suffer from deep shame who have herpes. For me, it was an ailment

---

[7] "False pregnancy," Wikipedia, last modified October 3, 2022, https://en.wikipedia.org/wiki/False_pregnancy.

[8] "Genital Herpes," CDC Detailed Fact Sheet, Centers for Disease Control, accessed August 21, 2022, https://www.cdc.gov/std/herpes/stdfact-herpes-detailed.htm#ref1.

that I used to serve my bottom-shelf self-worth. See what we are battling against as survivors? It can be quite an untangling of layers, so don't judge yourself if you discover you don't actually have the issues you have been carrying with you for so long. Do not punish yourself for losing time treating ghost ailments. You were given those burdens by abuse, not your own doing of your mind, body, and spirit.

I soon manifested new physical ailments. My body had been violated since infancy, so there was a lot of psychic and cellular programming to reverse. I was going to take my body back, but first I had to reclaim it.

Achalasia

In 2015, three months after telling my family about the abuse, I developed a constant nervous feeling in the back of my throat, as if acid reflux and anxiety collided and were tap dancing on my esophagus. Nervous, jittery twinges on my trachea. Then I couldn't swallow food properly. A piece of peanut butter toast with coffee needed four glasses of water to get each bite down. I was perplexed by this condition but chalked it up to anxiety and part of getting sober. I shared my story about these severe manifestations at AA meetings. I realize now that while I absolutely love AA, it was not the right place to be vetting my health. I didn't seek any other counsel. I started to limit what I could eat, and I dropped weight.

My best course of action for my throat affliction was to intellectualize it in my head. I would think to myself, *I am all alone and not with God, because where was he when my body was doing weird stuff when I was a little girl and being touched?*

One day, I was teaching kindergarten when I choked so hard on a piece of bagel that I thought I was going to vomit into the trash can in front of twenty-three kids. My throat constricted shut, and I was helpless, suspended in time to when I was five years old—the epicenter of my trauma. Thankfully, the kids were working on a craft project at their tables, so I struggled to swallow the lodged bite of bagel. Tears welled up in my eyes and burned hot down my cheeks. Eventually, I burped up enough bile and coughed my throat raw enough to open the passage up. I was exhausted and scared. I thought, *I don't think I can eat anymore.*

My body was no longer getting the nutrients it needed. It was impossible when all I would eat in a day was a Clif Bar and a fruit drink. I was nursing a lump on my chin that appeared after a bad flu (shortly after I told my mom about the abuse. Coincidence?). I finally researched and found out the lump was an abscess. Other definitions were a boil or a carbuncle. In Louise Hay's book, *You Can Heal Your Life,* she attributes an abscess to "fermenting thoughts over hurts, slights, and revenge."[9] A *carbunkle* is described as "poisonous anger about personal injustices."[10] She also pinpoints ailments on the left side of the body as "representing receptivity, taking in, feminine energy, women, the mother."[11] When the pustule on my face started pounding, I finally made an appointment to see my doctor.

"Oh God, Kim, you don't look good," my doctor said as she looked at me with grave concern. "What took you so long to come in?"

I looked in the mirror and saw what I had become: a gaunt, thin woman with a huge bump on her chin. When it comes to abuse, there aren't many ways to look at yourself in the mirror except, "Am I pretty enough to be objectified?" Or "I hate myself so much that I am going to pick at my face and scar it so I can be the damaged reflection I believe I am."

---

[9] Hay, *You Can Heal Your Life,* 146.

[10] Hay, 159.

[11] Hay, 182.

The abscess developed into streptococcus that had spread into my bloodstream, and the bacteria was slowly poisoning me and attacking my body. I knew this was indicative of the trauma oozing out. I finally got honest about not eating and choking. She prescribed me antibiotics and recommended a throat x-ray. I scheduled one and then canceled it. My denial was so thick. I did not want to have any medical treatments. As a baby, I had been opened up twice for a urethral dilation (stretching of the urethra). When I was pregnant, I had two C-sections, an umbilical hernia after my second baby, and then there was the invasive sexual abuse. I was hesitant to trust anyone with my body. Despite really loving my doctor, I was also scared I was dying just as I was finally getting my shit together.

I went to work the next day because I needed somewhere to go. I went to therapy and cried and screamed. I told my body— assured it—that I no longer needed to contain these deep secrets and that I was setting them free. These ailments were the last line of defense against the toxic secrets of shame oozing out of me. The nastiness of the trauma in my body, deep within my cells, wanted out. I got fierce about healing my body on my own. I was a survivor, right? No weird ailment was going to hold me back from life again. I was taking charge. So I decided to learn how to live a productive life on a liquid diet. God was completely absent from this decision.

I researched the best way to get nutrients into your body through liquid. Despite the fact that I was throwing up all over myself in the middle of the night, I devised a clever plan of self-will. New restrictions were implemented. No eating after five o'clock. No more chocolate. I stopped exercising to keep my calorie count in check. I had a friend come over and elevate my bed with bricks at an angle so my throat wouldn't burn while I slept. I became a connoisseur of pureed soups and veggie and fruit smoothies, and I finally had four nights of amazing sleep with my elevated bed. I could live this way! I would still periodically Google "acid reflux," but there were aspects of that condition that did not apply to what I was experiencing. My thoughts would wander to throat cancer, which kept me from seeking real medical help.

I prayed to God for guidance, but I was not listening to his answers. I was listening to myself telling God what I wanted to hear. God was not interested in my plan. He was ready to take me to a higher place.

I wish I could say this didn't go on much longer and I got smarter, but I was still untangling many crossed messages about the value of my body. I was afraid I'd made it this far only to die. I went to an intuitive healer for answers. Dave would touch points on my body and then stand across the room. I would twitch and release in the energy field. It was brilliant to feel the deeply embedded repression begin to wash away. During one session, I saw the brightest light inside of me—it radiated from my heart. I witnessed my ability to be big and bold and beautiful. I was totally freaked out. I could tell the real me was trapped inside my body and wanted out. My true adult soul was being held captive by a pissed-off, revengeful, scared little girl.

It was calming to be with a man who physically connected with me to help me heal, but we were not sexual. His healing helped me rewrite the trauma by reconnecting me to my body. He was helping me get over the fear of the ailment that was invading my body. He realigned my body in a new way that was completely free of the old constraints. I trusted him when I closed my eyes and lay on my couch, and he touched just the tops of my toes. He used EFT (Emotional Freedom Technique) in his practice, which involves tapping points on your body to release physical pain or emotional distress. I tapped on buried grief that had turned into vigilant anger. Dave taught me that what my truth was one day may not be my truth tomorrow.

I went back to my doctor and confessed I had never had the x-rays on my throat done. I could no longer ignore that I weighed 105 pounds. I was 125 pounds nine months prior—my weight my whole adult life. She took one look at me and said, "You need to see a gastroenterologist immediately. I am going to make a personal call to get you in to see him as soon as possible. This is serious. You may end up on a feeding tube."

I couldn't believe it, and I was also so incredibly grateful to her and the gastroenterologist who had diagnosed me with achalasia. I burst into tears when he called me with this diagnosis. "What the hell is that?" I said, tears streaming down my face.

"Well, it's a rare autoimmune disorder where your esophagus loses its motility."

"Why? Why now?" I said.

"There's no rhyme or reason for it," the doctor said. "It just happens to people your age."

On that call, Adult Kim took over for the scared little girl and told her the situation was going to be okay. We now had answers . . . and solutions. I was no longer a victim. I was in charge of my body as a grown adult. It wasn't shocking that my throat shut down after I faced the abuse. Now I needed to reclaim my body as an adult from the frightened child in the corner who had been violated. It took choking and gagging to come to that realization and own it. *The devil screams the loudest right before he dies.*

The first test I had to endure was an esophageal manometry test, which measures the lack of motility in the esophagus. My surgeon revealed later that he never tells patients just how hideous this test is because no one would go through with it. According to the technician who was administering the test, 50 percent of people abort it in the middle and don't get the surgery approved. I am so proud I made it through, but it was an act of sheer willpower.

My friend Jane accompanied me to the test because I had learned through my twelve-step recovery to not do anything alone. I am so glad she was there. The technician threaded a four-foot-long metal tube up my nose, down my throat, and into my stomach. There is no anesthetic administered because you need to be awake to swallow. They sealed the end of the tube to my face with a Hannibal Lecter-style mask and poured liquid down my throat. I couldn't swallow food or liquids, so it just pooled there, and I gagged and choked and pounded my heels on the table and cried out for it to stop. Jane said it took everything she had to stay in the room. It was unbearable to watch. A banana-like goo followed the water, and I choked and gagged on that substance for ten minutes. I was scared, but I was strong. This was part of taking back my life, and I was not going to let any part of me quit. One of the leading experts in the country for achalasia confirmed I had stage-one achalasia. Within two weeks I was having surgery to repair my esophagus.

Throughout this process, I learned that abuse survivors have a high tolerance to endure stress and trauma, which helps us manifest a bigger life. We can walk through more real-life shit. We have a deeper capacity to stand strong in the face of adversity, fear, or uncomfortable growth. This is one of our blessings from the abuse.

YOUR AILMENTS INVENTORY

It's important to pay attention to your body and start to emerge out of denial about what could be an ailment—real or manifested—and how you can better care for yourself. You need to mentally and physically stay in reality.

Consider the following questions:

- When was the last time you had a routine checkup? For women, this also includes an ob/gyn appointment. Also, do you get regular STD testing if you have multiple partners?

- How often do you see specialists for specific conditions that bother you? Do you have a mole on your face that is getting bigger? Have you been extra dizzy lately and are almost passing out on a regular basis?

- Make a list of all the ailments you currently have and fight off the voices that judge you of being a complainer or weak. Make a list of everything that hurts, from a sore toe to back pain. Get very honest about your body so you can start to see patterns and consider getting help.

If you have a notion that you may be neglecting your self-care but are still not convinced, read on. Before I got better, I experienced extreme denial of my illnesses and radically abandoned myself and my needs. I wouldn't wish this path on any other survivor.

SURGERY AS A SURVIVOR

Part of taking back your body is understanding the support and mindset you may need to assure yourself that you are safe when undergoing invasive procedures. You have been violated in abuse, and there is a very good chance that when you need a surgery, whether inpatient or outpatient, you will be triggered by how powerless you are. The positive aspect of this scenario is that you can heal and grow if you take charge of your surroundings, ask questions to the providers, and don't go into any procedure blindly. When we were abused, we had a lot of confusion. We don't need to be confused about our bodies anymore. We get to be the CEOs of our bodies!

The Universe is profoundly interesting if you are open to healing on all levels, physically and mentally. My mom insisted on flying out to California to take care of me during the week I was having surgery for the achalasia. I allowed her to come, but I promised myself that I would be completely honest with everyone at the surgery if I was scared. I needed a voice because I never had one as a child, with the urethra surgery, the abuse, or when my first daughter was born and there were all kinds of complications due to a failed cervix. For this surgery, I would cry if I needed to, and I wouldn't be a quiet victim like the abused child. That mode was done. I told my mom I was scared while we waited in the prep room for the anesthesiologist. I cried. She did the best she could to console me. She did not try to shut me down, and she stuck in there with me. It was not about her. It was about me fully revealing who I was. I am very sensitive to anesthesia, so when they gave me Dilaudid to just "mellow me out" before the big stuff, I passed out completely.

After the surgery, my mom told me what had happened. "While you were still deep under in the operating room," she said, "you sat up and started shrieking and yelling, 'I'm scared, I'm scared!'"

"Really?" I said, tickled pink at my commitment to self-expression in a time of great invasion.

"Yes," she said, shifting a bit uncomfortably in her chair. "None of the nurses knew what to do with you. Frankly, it was quite freaky."

"Well, I'm sorry you had to experience that," I said, although I wasn't sorry at all. I sat back in my bed, grinning from ear to ear. I had done exactly what I wanted. I had a goddamn voice. I had spoken up and spoken out, and I didn't give a shit what it looked like to anyone. In fact, I know now that I wasn't just speaking to the nurses and doctors. I was speaking to my mother about those surgeries to stretch my urethra when I was a child. I was taking back my body, which was not only affected by that past medical abuse, but also the incest that was occurring in my home with my father.

Are you preparing for any surgeries? If so, you don't have to be a trooper who just gets the paperwork done while ignoring your fears and feelings. I constantly hear stories from survivors who are about to undergo invasive procedures and think they can drive themselves home. They don't want to bother anyone with their care. Know this: you don't have to be alone. Learn to ask for help when you need it.

Here are a few tips to help you prepare for any type of surgery so you don't have to be alone:

- Ask someone who is gentle, compassionate, and organized to be your advocate. Hospitals are chaotic places, and you need someone to advocate for your needs, especially if you are on medications or bedridden.

- Discuss your concerns and fears about the procedure with your friends or confidants, no matter how irrational they may sound. I once was so traumatized by an endometrial biopsy that I almost passed out in the office and sobbed for an hour to my therapist in my car. Don't think you have to be so strong and not allow yourself to experience fear, which is old trauma resurfacing.

- Find a spiritual connection to your body through meditation, a massage before the procedure, or loving affirmations. You and your body are partners, not adversaries.

HEALING AFTER SURGERY

Recovery from the surgery was another trial of how proactive I could be with knowing my body. I had abused it for so long with drugs and alcohol to numb myself. Now I was feeling everything, and I was still in the early years of uncovering more about the abuse memories and my feelings.

Having surgery is one hurdle to overcome, but then you have to deal with coming off the drugs or getting off a catheter. The epidural they kept in me for three days really messed up my digestive system. I got severely constipated, and if you are nodding your head, you know what that means in terms of control and the body as a survivor. Holding on to the poop inside is a tiny act of power. I did it as a kid to prove to myself that I had some control over my body (to my detriment), and now the constipation was re-triggering the body panic. Two weeks after the surgery, I became a little manic with laxatives, buying everything Rite Aid sold, because I was desperate to release myself from this age-old cycle. Then a friend told me I was acting addictive with them. Could I just chill out and trust my body? The women around me were holding me up so high and strong to reclaim my body. But I was so scared that I had lost control of my body again after going through so much to get it back physically, mentally, and spiritually.

A girlfriend in recovery referred an amazing colonic clinic in Los Angeles, and the practitioner guided me through two one-hour sessions of release. As she massaged my arms and hands, she told me I would be able to have my body back, but I needed to be a partner with it and not fight it. It was profoundly healing, and after a few months, I started to have a regular experience with my body again. I had almost immediately gained all the lost weight back, and I was stunned to see that I was the same weight as I was before the achalasia, but without the muscle tone I was accustomed to. I started practicing hatha yoga and stopped running so fast and hard. I enjoyed walks in the middle of the day for perspective and tension release instead of wanting to look hot in jeans. After about a year, I was able to reconnect with my body in a new way.

Whatever physical trials you have faced in your recovery from abuse, the best part of the journey is learning to love and appreciate your body and wanting to be healthy for your children, your friends, and to pursue your dreams as the new you. Part of this awareness is no longer denying that future medical procedures may cause you heightened levels of trauma. Dental procedures, such as root canals, can be triggering because of their invasive nature. I've had challenges with the insertion of an IUD. You don't have to be blindsided by your reaction to these experiences if you don't live in denial about what you can handle as a survivor.

Our body carries us around. We need to love it and honor it. Our love for our body is connected to our ultimate soulful happiness. That said, not everything that happens to us in recovery aligns directly to the abuse. You don't want to make excuses for not participating in an activity or a procedure that can help and heal you. It also does you no good to dwell on the trauma in your body. Just know that you are not alone in feeling uncomfortable in your body. Our adult selves can finally take back our bodies from the little children we are inside. They can finally rest assured that we are going to take care of them now.

THOUGHT-PROVOKING QUESTIONS

Is there any ailment you are dealing with right now that you are not seeing a specialist or a doctor about? Get honest with how long you have been struggling with this ailment, and then consider seeing someone (and not Dr. Google!).

Do you consider routine medical checkups as positive or negative for your body? Do you trust your caregivers, or are you seeing someone who you suspect is not doing as good a job as you deserve?

What medical treatments have you received since the abuse? Write about your experience and describe in vivid detail what you recall seeing and perceiving.

Chapter 9

GENERATIONAL ABUSE

My commitment to ending the rage that was instilled in me by generational abuse was not easy, but the end product of a happy, peaceful home (most of the time) was worth the painful unraveling of my anger. I knew no one in my children's home would ever sexually abuse them, but as I discuss in this chapter, abuse is not just sexual. I had to take long, hard looks in the mirror about my abusive, angry behavior. In abuse recovery, I had to explore the generational roots of my anger, as well as the lifetime of self-loathing that lay beneath the surface. Growing up, the people in my family didn't talk about their feelings unless they were yelling at someone or cutting them out of their lives. It was hard love.

I had to swallow all of the raging I had done at my children when they were young while making efforts to change our generational history. I had to cope with my guilt and sorrows while learning to create a loving environment where we did not deny that rage had existed—doing so would just perpetuate the denial and lies.

When I came to terms with abuse denial, I felt the pressure to quickly change my angry and violent behavior around my young children. Repressed abuse evokes ire, especially if you witnessed rage during the years you were abused. If you judge yourself for still having angry outbursts despite coming to terms with the abuse, I can assure you that if you commit to doing the deeper work, this anger will one day be completely gone. We can be the generation that brings about change by teaching our children that there is a different way to be seen and heard. You will have to be more mindful of the potential triggers when you feel overextended and have not given yourself love and grace. I had been at 85 percent for many years, and that 15 percent when I could still rage would cause me a lot of despair. But I knew if I committed to conquering my rage and prayed to God that I could love myself enough to change, it would dissipate.

A reaction trigger was planted in me by generations of people who had no coping mechanisms for their frustrations and feelings. We keep going until we crack. We have no self-love, so we go until we lose it on others. We adopt the personas of our family's origin because we've been buried in denial and don't know who we are. Before I knew about and dealt with my sexual abuse, my sadness manifested into anger. I was always a fighter when it came to men: with my dad, boyfriends, cab drivers, men on movie sets, and anyone who didn't behave according to my standards. I beat up on computers and cars. I didn't know what was wrong with me. I knew I hated everything around me and everything inside me, but marijuana and alcohol bandaged my feelings on a temporary basis. That was what I knew growing up. People around me were angry, and I was angry that I couldn't tell anyone about the abuse. So there was a lot of anger and no love or softness. I spent most of my adult life thinking I wasn't kind or soft. I was convinced I was a tough-love badass. Today, I have learned to communicate with all the parts of who I am, but it has taken time and work. I can still be forward and forthright, but that is because I'm stepping into my own essence of self, not the generations before me. You, too, can find a way out of anger and stop yelling at those around you. You can open yourself to love.

GETTING HONEST ABOUT SHAME

Depending on your upbringing, you could be engaging in acts

of neglect, silent treatment, biting sarcasm, or criticism. These are learned coping mechanisms as a result of how you were treated. Your history of sexual or physical abuse and trauma can be a gateway to inappropriate parenting. There are no excuses if you behave in a harmful or dangerous way to your children, regardless of whether their behavior needs course correction. Get better so you can change the legacy. That act is on you.

I walked through a dark, seemingly endless forest of abuse to discover that the first real love I could ever feel deep in my heart was for my children. I was forty-six years old, sober, and frightened of how deeply I was capable of loving. I went to my women's AA meeting and cried out of shame because I had never known true love in my life. I had many friends, husbands, and boyfriends, yet I never truly let them in because my heart had been shut down from the abuse. I felt like I had never really met anyone at a deep level of intimacy and trust because I wasn't safe to be around. I didn't want to treat my children with sarcasm. I saw how biting it was, and I had to learn new parenting skills to avoid the behaviors that stemmed from my own self-loathing from the abuse.

My bond with my children started to show itself in its power and intimacy because I opened my eyes to loving myself. Loving them reaches depths that are still beyond my limited understanding. The feelings I have when I give my complete time and attention to them are so profound. I am proud of myself. I am finally living like a responsible, healed adult who can safely parent two children rather than a terribly frightened, tormented inner child who runs the show.

I wish I could say there wasn't residual fallout, but it took my older daughter a year into my recovery to stop flinching if I moved too quickly or to realize I was not being sarcastic. My father had taught me these domination and control tactics. As I unraveled the abuse, my teen daughter and I started to talk about how my behavior affected her. I made no justifications about what had happened. *Yes, I grabbed you. Yes, I screamed in your face. Yes, I bet it was really scary.* No denying. No justifying. I just had to get better and cope with my raging inner child.

I would not only be hurtful to my children. In denial, I would discard people. I was cold to the humanness of others. I had no connection with myself, so how could I connect with someone else?

I want to emphasize that this type of behavior does stop, but it takes work. Today, I don't waste time with regret because my kids love and need me on a daily basis, and I am showing up like a rock-star mom both logistically and emotionally. There are still days when I wonder what it must have been like for my firstborn, who was five years old at the time, to look into my deadened eyes as I screamed in colorful rage. She was scared, just as I had feared my father or my mother, both of whom could be so angry, hard, and unforgiving. As a parent, I would go into a trance and not be present. I would suddenly be in the mindset of the apathetic abuser. After raging, I would provide comfort. I would swear my love and that I would be kinder the next time she misbehaved. While I did not sexually abuse anyone, I took on that same monstrous behavior of my sexual abuser. My angry, abused subconscious was not ready to change. I had no idea how futile it was.

While people say raising a teen is challenging, I can't use that excuse in conflict. When my older daughter tells me to shut up, I have a trigger that makes me want to grab her and silence her like I was once silenced. I know that makes no sense, especially since she and I are bonded and feel deep love. None of this is her fault. I love this child with every fiber of my motherly heart, but it takes effort to not physically react if I feel disrespected.

Retaliation is in my DNA, but I am gradually learning to control the trigger and lean into the peace and love that I feel most of the time. In any situation involving either of my children, I feel God's hand come in and lay it down. In my trauma blindness, God's loving presence reminds me that these are my beloved children who need me. I am their ultimate guide and teacher.

My teen is not a perpetrator. She is not the enemy. Yet, she has a long history of helping me get better when I had less control over my emotions and reactions. Since we have healed so much, she feels betrayed when an angry episode erupts that reminds her of my losing control when she was little. She told me this one day after we fought and I took her phone. I was devastated. How can I create an environment that fosters betrayal for a kid who has only been on this earth for sixteen years? That cut to the core, but I am grateful she told me. I felt betrayed by my mother, and I was carrying that feeling. The difference is that my daughter trusts that she can tell me she feels betrayed and that I will listen. I never said anything like that to my mom because she would have either invalidated it, taken it personally and held it against me, or yelled at me. I didn't learn to communicate with anyone when I was younger.

I felt all powerful when I lashed out at my young kids or my ex-husband, but I really had no power in my life. I had been rendered so powerless since infancy when the abuse began. I was clawing for some kind of truth that didn't exist. It made the little monster inside me—the inner child monster—angrier and angrier. I didn't have the courage to wonder what was wrong with me until my dad died and I left my second marriage. I don't suggest that anyone should clean house with their family in order to recover from sexual abuse, but that was how my story played out. The denial was so thick. I had no choice but to go through recovery alone to really see the whole history. It had to be done for my children. Every time I grabbed my daughter's arm too tightly or pushed my little one because she wouldn't stop crying, I grew more deep hate for myself. The cycle of abuse had to end.

Today, my children trust me because I have worked through the shame. Occasionally, when my kids see me getting worked up about a mess in the house, they'll warn me. "Mom, you are getting aggressive. Slow it down." I listen. I check myself. I ask, "What am I afraid of in this moment that will go wrong?" I get perspective. Life is too short to be hyped up. Of course, I am the authority figure and parent my kids for their best interest, but there is a fine line that should not be crossed. We don't own our children. They are a blessing and not here on this earth to be dominated. They are trapped in our homes and are innocent to our behavior. Being an abuse survivor really showed me how to respect my children, and I am grateful for this revelation. I know this is not the same for many parents, but maybe one day they will realize why there is so much dysfunction in their family legacy.

TOOLS TO TALK

We learn from our communication with our parents. If your parent was an abuser and your family was complicit, think about the work you will need to do as an adult to learn to communicate. Be open about what happened in your family while you were in abuse denial, but don't let guilt prevent you from getting better with how you express your anger. Anger is a human emotion when applied to a rational context of communication. Just don't abuse it.

You want a good life? Learn to talk.

Here are some tools I use to help me communicate better with my daughters, but you can use them with a spouse, siblings, or even roommates.

Talk: Use a talking stick to communicate. Only the person holding the talking stick can speak, so this allows their voice to be heard by an active, listening audience. Once someone is holding the talking stick in their hand, watch out! You can't get them to stop sharing because they feel empowered. The talking stick can be any object—a wooden spoon or even a drumstick. Have fun and decorate the stick with your children.

Wait: The best time to hash out a heated and contentious situation is not in the epicenter of the conflict. You need to wait it out. Give it at least twenty-four hours. For example, you can say, "I don't want to go to bed mad, but I think we all may have a better perspective in the morning."

Walk: Go for a walk and rage out loud at the open air or yell in a basement. Don't just tell yourself you shouldn't be angry. That condemning self-judgment only represses you further and denies you a voice that is agitated.

I am so grateful that the abusive legacy ends with my daughters thanks to my acceptance of my part. That is because I have learned to listen and be open with communicating my feelings.

CALMING THE MONSTER WITHIN

Two years into recovery, as I was unraveling the acts of sexual abuse and how I had survived the world as a victim, I realized that I was simply reenacting the monster that attacked me when I was little and helpless. The monster had silenced my voice. When my older daughter was younger, I would silence her cries by clamping my hand over her mouth, even when it was a little too long and she gasped for breath. When she wouldn't go to bed, I would scream and leave in a rage with a door slam. I am sure my daughter would shiver in her bed.

I lost control of the rage that grew inside me. I would lose perspective of a smaller creature who needed my love and protection. It is sad I didn't understand it then. I had a repressed secret. I was angry and frustrated a lot. Thank God I also created lots of very happy memories with my children, but that does not make up for screaming at them. A switch would be flipped. When I told people, "Boy, I get really angry sometimes with my kids," they would shake their heads and agree and sympathize. "Parenting little ones can take you to the edge," they would say, but inside I was screaming. *No, you don't understand. The way I feel toward them is loathsome. Can someone tell me to stop?*

In 2011, I had my first messenger. This was a year before I had the abuse dream. I had just split up with my second husband and my kids' father. I was so enraged and bitter. My seven-year-old daughter didn't want to get out of the car to go to a Buddhist chant on New Year's Day (what kid would want to go?), and I pulled her out of the car with such force that she smacked her forehead. I recalled having no feeling about it. Later, I thought, *I am like a man who abuses his wife, cleans it up, and then loves her again, and so she stays . . . but my kids don't have the choice to leave. They are stuck with me.* I was so frightened and stunned by this thought. I told my Al-Anon sponsor about what happened.

She was the first person to ever say to me, "Kim, you are raging against your children, and it is not okay. It could get worse. It is not acceptable, and you have to stop today."

The tone of her voice scared me. I knew she was right. I could not believe the monster I was becoming. I was so confused about how I could be a consistently safe, warm, and caring mother most of the time, but then this monster would erupt. I made a vow right then and there to never lay a single finger on my kids or scream at them.

For a little while, I did a lot better. There was an incident in the public library that sent me into a rageful tailspin. The tedium and monotony of having sole custody of my children, combined with my lack of emotional stability, led me to believe I had lost my phone in the library. I screamed at my three-year-old to get out of the car. I was blind with rage and wasn't thinking clearly about her fear in that moment. I stormed into the library, swearing and yelling, and found the phone. I drove home quivering in a simmering rage. If either child tried to talk to me, I told them I was so angry I couldn't even speak. They had done nothing wrong.

I can't even believe I had gone to such frightening depths. If that happened today, I am so grateful to say I would be calm and serene. While I don't really lose stuff anymore, I surely don't blame my daughters. I raised two little girls to be confident bigger girls who love themselves. Today, they feel the radiation of my own self-love, assurance, confidence, and humor. I am taking back my life without it having to be a raging, bitter act.

FACE DENIAL AND STOP THE CYCLE

If you are struggling with anger issues and you hate yourself for it, you can get well. I recovered, and now my life with my children includes healthy boundaries, and the love and communication is deep and honest. For some people, anger management is an option. I engaged in a Listening Partnership[12] with a friend who was also a therapist. She had read a fascinating study about how listening partnerships give people space to share, and there are certain ways to touch the other person to assure them that it was not invasive. For several weeks, my friend sat on my couch

[12] Shaun Casey, "12 Ways to Make Time for Listening Partnerships (And Make Parenting Easier)," Hand in Hand Parenting, November 21, 2021, https://www.handinhandparenting.org/2021/11/12-ways-to-make-time-for-listening-partnerships-and-make-parenting-easier/.

and listened to me cry and rage, and then I did the same for her. While we both felt incredibly gutted after these sessions, we did not bring that venting to our kids.

Some people don't know why they may manhandle their children. It may not be evident that there was abuse in their past, or they're aware of the abuse but don't believe that is why they are rough with their children. Doing inner child work helped me approach my anger. When I faced the fact that my inner little girl was repressed and was going to rage until she got the attention and acknowledgment to heal, I started to change my behavior in a radical way for the first time. My inner little girl was not going to allow me to give unconditional love to my complaining, consuming, joyfully perfect little children until her complaints from the past were heard and she was healed. She was going to use the unrealized, unformed adult me as a vessel to minimize my children until her time in the sun was had. She was a terror and a tyrant. I talk more about inner child work in chapter 11.

If you are abusing your children physically, verbally, or sexually, you need to stop. I can't stress enough what the long-term emotional repercussions could be for you and your children. Child Protective Services (CPS) can take your children away and put them into foster care. Our system in the United States will not necessarily put your children in a loving family. They could end up in a group home and be subjected to far more torment. Am I scaring you? I hope so, because there were times when my kids were just crying because they were tired or frustrated, and I worried my neighbors would call CPS. Even though I was getting my anger in check and healing my family, I still felt shame for a long time after.

In the early days of my recovery, I called a woman in AA who had forty years of sobriety. I caught a small glimpse of the old me earlier that morning when my younger daughter and I were fighting. She didn't want to go to school and was lying on the bathroom floor. I was yelling at her, and she was yelling at me. I was out of options, so I physically pulled her up by her shirt. The shirt sleeve left a mark on her arm, and she was plunged into despair. I was devastated because I thought this chapter of my life had closed.

After my sober friend calmed me down by getting me to laugh about her own mishaps with her child, she said, "Kim, you don't want that life anymore. You know that. You don't have that life today. You are sober and a wonderful mother. But you got scared. Do you want to be in sparring matches with your children?"

"No, not at all," I rasped out between sniffles.

"Then this is what you say to your children in a calm voice: 'There is no yelling at Mommy,' and then you don't yell either. You tell your children that there will be no more yelling in the house. They can pound their pillows and scream outside, but not in the house. And your daughter goes to school on time or she is marked tardy."

I loved this advice, so the next time one of my daughters screamed at me, I calmly said, "There is no screaming at Mommy." I kept repeating this mantra while keeping an eye on her. Then I asked her what was making her so mad.

My young daughter, sensing I was a loving presence, accessed enough courage to admit she was sad, and she didn't know what to do about her feelings because she didn't know why they were there. I sat on the floor with her and held her because I completely related. I spent my whole life raging because of a locked-away sadness I was not allowed to feel when I was her age. I had a dark secret and no one to tell and no one to hold me. I was an angry little monster.

I told my daughter that when we don't talk about our sad

feelings, they can manifest into anger, and that was what was happening to her.

I asked her, "What does the sadness feel like?"

She said, "It's like when you are going to sneeze but you can't, and you hold it back and it just waits there." It felt like that in the pit of her stomach. I held her as she let out a few sobs and then it was over.

Now when my children and I snuggle together and watch movies, my eyes brim with tears of gratitude to God for saving us. I spend as much time as I can with them. I have taken them to Spain, Mexico, New York City, and Paris. I have been there every weekend for track meets, lacrosse games, plays, and debates. I am available and responsible and proud of my parenting. Most of all, I don't rage at them. I am grateful that I stopped my rageful behavior and was able to break the family pattern. God helped me find freedom from the abuse and the courage to take these painful experiences and grow. To not perpetuate the hard, angry, inner-child feelings on my children anymore. To love so deeply that sometimes I think I am going to burst. Eventually, that high of love gets mellowed out—not in a bad, apathetic way, but it becomes your new norm, and it isn't another form of an addictive high that can burn out.

I know this is brutally painful, but if you have been abusive to your children as an unrecovered abuse survivor, you need to dislodge old patterning so you can cut the cord and stop passing this behavior down to future generations. Your shame is less important than ending the history of abuse. Take action to stop the abuse. Go to therapy, talk to friends, or go to a support group—do whatever you need to stop abusing your children.

DEEPER EXPLORATION OF RAGE

If there is a mad, mad monster inside of you that is screaming to get out, I am here to confirm once again that it can stop. You can caress with those hands instead of repress. One of the key tools for confronting rage is educating yourself about the range of emotions you can have when in conflict and negotiation with others. How have you avoided expressing your needs? When we are silent about what we want and need, it can trigger a powerlessness that leads to rage.

Here are some concepts to explore about rage:

Expectations

An expectation is really a premeditated judgment. You want someone to behave in a certain way so you can get the payoff you need. I am not saying we can't expect people to fulfill their obligations or jobs, but we can attach meaning to our friends, loved ones, or coworkers' actions. Lower your expectations for a while so you can then find the people in your life who consistently show up or behave in a way that meets your expectations.

Judgment

How often do you judge yourself and others? Do you look at how a person may process an experience and feel a sense of loathing about them? When we judge ourselves and think we are not enough, we can project that outward to avoid having to sit with how bad we feel about ourselves. If you say loving affirmations, it will soften you inside so you can tap into that deeper part of acceptance.

Justification

I hate to say it, but sexual abuse recovery can lead to a sense of entitlement or justification. There was a woman in AA meetings who used to say, "Don't you know who I am? Don't you know what I have been through?" These are not excuses to drop the ball in your life and then take it out on others when they confront your behavior. If you said you were going to show up on time, show up. If you made a promise to do a job, do it. Don't expect everyone to let you off the hook because you were abused. That's irresponsible. And don't get pissed off about it. It's not fair to others or yourself.

Here's the truth. There may be times when you really just need to smash shit or have a good rage session in the privacy of your home when no one else is around. Embrace that release and don't stuff it in. There are rage rooms you can rent out where you are given a bucket of plates and glasses to smash on the walls. You can even throw axes at targets. Do it. Get it out of your system, but at the same time, keep up the inner work.

When you are no longer in denial about your inner rage, you can give yourself an opportunity to start living for the first time in the gracious middle. That middle state allows you to negotiate and understand other communication tools, such as what you can do when your expectations haven't been met, or when you feel judged or are judging others. You have the opportunity to delve deeper into your frustration, sadness, and loss without resorting to rage. We say in recovery, "Are you hungry, angry, lonely, or tired?" Check in with yourself first before you check out and end up in a blind rage. We have alienated ourselves from intimacy and love for so long. When we open ourselves up to a bigger life, we can practice forgiving ourselves and others.

THOUGHT-PROVOKING QUESTIONS

Have you raged on people in your life while you were repressing your abuse secret? Now that you are no longer in denial about the abuse, how has that anger presented itself in your life?

How do you treat the people you love in your life? Your children? Your siblings? Your spouse? Do you yell? Do you understand why you are yelling? Write down the abusive terms or insults you may say over and over again. They can reveal how you actually feel about yourself.

Do you believe it is possible to have healthy anger? Anger is a sign that our boundaries and intentions are out of balance. Where can you course correct to be in a better state of peace?

Chapter 10
ENERGY

If we have been abused as children, we take on the intrusive energy of the abuser. Abuse is imbalanced. One person takes while the other person is taken from. There is no reciprocity.

When we are abused, someone takes power over our energy source. Your energy is pure and lovely when you are a child, but abuse causes you to disassociate and splinter. Your energy, which may have been naturally balanced at birth, is now frenetic. Many survivors don't know why they feel deliriously happy one minute and morose and sad the next. It's the pendulum swing of unbalanced energy. There is an entire self-help industry built on healers because people want to feel balanced and whole now more than ever. If your energy is balanced, you can wake up every day feeling in touch with who you are, free from the constraints of denial and the people who oppressed you.

Abuse survivors can be loners. Getting too close to others can feel energetically unsafe. Throughout my life, I have left friend groups or communities and never spoke to anyone in the group again. At first, I thought this was just a happenstance of my nomadic lifestyle, but I realized that most people have some kind of longevity with others. While I found peace in the fact that I had two girlfriends from college, I had no clue where anyone I had shared life with for the last fifty years was. I moved on quickly from any kind of long-term energy exchange because it was too painful to yearn for anyone, and it was easier to say goodbye and move on to the next.

I had friends in college I never saw again. Friends in New

York City whom I rarely saw except for one gal on Facebook. I had a community in Los Angeles, but that fell by the wayside when I stopped making movies and doing drugs. I then had a community in San Jose at my daughter's Jewish Israeli preschool, but that wasn't sustainable because I couldn't join the synagogue and we moved again. I had a small group of mom friends in Berkeley, but we moved back to Los Angeles after my second child was born. Even in early abuse recovery, I had a circle of sober friends that I now barely talk to aside from one or two. When I went deeper into self-exploration, I found that I wanted to have more long-lasting friendships that sustained time, but I had to put down my masculine wall of never showing my feelings or flaws. I had to start being honest about who I was so I could attract more long-lasting friends. The two friends I have had for thirty years have remained in my life because they have seen me at my worst. I have told them my deepest and darkest secrets, and they have shared theirs. The energy exchanges have been even.

To thrive as abuse survivors, understanding energetic balance is essential. Our energy is what drives us to live and love, succeed, and grow.

FEMININE VERSUS MASCULINE ENERGY

Throughout my life, I was completely disconnected from my female energy. Because the abuse groomed me to be a provider, a dominant masculine energy shut down the pissed-off little girl inside of me from healing. In relationships, I took on "traditional" male roles, where I was the one complaining about not having enough sex (this was my worth). In my twenties, intimacy with female friends meant going to clubs and doing drugs (I'm so fun!). I didn't practice self-care in a feminine way, such as nurturing soft feelings or shaping who I was as a woman who could relax, be taken care of, or allow my creative side to naturally evolve. At the same time, I would abandon any gut instinct to sit back, watch, and access what might be good or bad for my life. I needed a take-charge mentality of all masculine components to survive in my life.

When I was twenty-five, I felt old inside and already around the block, but I couldn't stop driving forward. I was cultivating the capacity for a deeper anger and hardness, which would not be evident until my second marriage, progressive alcoholism, and having children. I got facials every six weeks to feel more "feminine," but I spent the entire time complaining about my husband to the aesthetician. I felt like I deserved these skincare products and facials because, damn it, I was a woman. But I didn't feel like a woman. I don't think I even thought like a woman.

When you have been abused, your feminine and masculine power is taken away simultaneously. The feminine side is abused, and the masculine side is too weak to fight back. Feminine power is a hot topic these days. How we stand in it, how we dress for it, and how we speak about it without being too masculine. How can you be feminine and still be powerful, and what does that power mean? Sure, we all love a good estrogen-filled fist-pumping women's empowerment conference to tap into our feminine power, but that is not the work we are doing here. We are untangling ourselves from a perpetrator who had become our emotional captor. Some women have learned to be feminine in their power. I have always wanted to know their secret.

Our soul holds both our feminine and masculine sides, and they are both beautiful. We need to be whole so we can express our feelings and avoid self-abandonment, which is what trauma survivors do with their detachment or disassociation. The self-abandoner believes "their needs and desires either cannot be met or *should* not be met . . ."[13]

So, what does it look like when we are leaning more masculine than feminine and our energy is out of balance? "Masculine energy is characterized by *doing* and *achieving* and is molded by logic and reason. The feminine is more *intuitive*, oriented toward receiving and allowing, and characterized by *being*."[14]

To advance their careers, many women have had to become more masculine and cut off the intuitive parts of themselves. Women are becoming burnt out, overextended, and cancer is on the rise. Heart attacks are the leading cause of death among women in America. So in the midst of all this noise, it can be difficult to face sexual abuse, which requires a gentler "return to the womb" approach.

HONORING FEMININE ENERGY

Living with feminine energy can be scary for abuse survivors because it often involves patience and trust. We are returning to the essence of the mother figure. What if you didn't get along with your mother, or if she was entangled in the abuse secrets or history? Or maybe you were abused by a mother or a stepmother. As a result, there will be a block in the feminine energy. Moving slowly and allowing circumstances to evolve requires tapping into an intuitive feminine self, which for many women is not a skill easily acquired.

---

[13] Brianna Johnson, "Are You a Chronic Self-Abandoner?" April 30, 2018, https://www.nami.org/Blogs/NAMI-Blog/April-2018/Are-You-a-Chronic-Self-Abandoner.

[14] Rena Satre Meloy, "Balancing Our Feminine and Masculine Energy," Pause, accessed August 8, 2022, https://www.pausemeditation.org/single-post/balancing-feminine-masculine-energy.

Giving Birth

I gave birth twice before I discovered I had been sexually abused and came out of denial. Looking back on those experiences, I see that I was too hard on myself and did not ask for what I needed. I was a mother creating a child, but I was doing so in a body with unresolved energy. Almost a decade later in recovery, I realized I needed to heal my womb and my inner feminine core.

My first delivery was a mess. After fifteen hours of a faulty cervix, I was drugged up even more and had a C-section. I never honored the fact that I went through extensive bodily invasion with my first child. I had so many drugs in my system. I didn't even meet her or nurse her until five hours after the birth.

My second baby was a scheduled C-section. I was taking no emotional or physical risks. I had a plan with a team of doctors. My baby was born in less than five minutes. I was able to be with her and nurse her on the spot. My one really feminine experience was efficient and effective.

To reconcile my feminine energy in the present, I needed to go back to the memories and experiences I had with childbirth. I discovered that the experiences had trapped some unresolved sadness in me. I talked through what was present for me energetically to a group of women who all needed to heal energetically. The power of healing with women is profound.

Female Friendships

When I first joined AA two years into my recovery, I went to women's meetings. I listened, watched, and learned from the other women there. I talked about not knowing what I wanted to wear or eat, and the confusion I felt about who I was sexually. As I ripped off the mask and showed up for myself each week vulnerable, messy, and honest, I started to feel love form in my heart like I had never felt before. I cried openly about how scared

I was at my ability to love my children. I was also terrified of my resentments, judgments, and how I used people to perpetuate my old story. Disheveled and raw, these women would listen to me and love me. They wore nice clothes, with their hair and makeup done, and I wanted to feel their ease, joy, and grace. They healed my long, dormant female insides by simply holding me in a strong, loving space and setting an example of stepping into their skin.

I even had a new female relationship with my AA sponsor that I hadn't had in a long time, if ever. She listened to me, and I listened to her. Nothing I did or said shocked her. She held me up as wonderful and powerful in the eyes of God. We began to have deep, funny conversations. She did my hair. I started to feel what it was like to really be a woman—not a damaged, abused little girl peering in from the outside at other women who appeared to be healthy and not abused. I wasn't messy, with holes and spilling all out. Sure, I would break down, but for the first time I started to do it as a whole woman. When I started dating, I borrowed a few dresses from her because I had nothing that was pretty, flouncy, and feminine. I surprised myself with my hair golden and curled, and my little dress and earrings, looking as feminine as I could.

I also hired a stylist because I hated shopping and was petrified of dressing the real me. She was so lovely. She went out and bought me some clothes. She rearranged my sparse closet. She encouraged me to think about jewelry and having a woman's wardrobe. She helped me organize my feminine side. I wanted to look nice when I left the house because it made me feel good. I wanted to be seen fully in all areas of my life. Even my daughters noticed when I dressed nice.

Honoring My Yoni

In order to align myself with my feminine energy, I was

abstinent during my second year of sobriety. I pretty much white-knuckled it, but it had to be done. I was three years into sexual abuse recovery and needed to be man-free to find my feminine side. My female friends all thought it was a great idea. They didn't even know the truth—that in all my interactions with women, I couldn't shake the feeling that I was nothing like them. I was rigid and uncomfortable, and I desired lightness and freedom. Sometimes, I almost felt like I was preying on women when I was socializing with them because I was such an outsider to my femininity. I thought I was gay for a brief spell, but I wasn't sexually attracted to women. I was definitely attracted to men. I just wanted desperately to feel feminine.

During my abstinence, crazy thoughts ran through my mind. I learned in SLAA that sexual anorexia is when you use abstinence as a defense mechanism against intimacy. *What if I become so sexually anorexic while developing new sexual values that I never have sex again until I meet "the one?"* I always had sex to lock a guy into a relationship or make an assumption that we were more serious than we really were. I hadn't ventured into one-night stands to meet my needs.

The abstinent period helped me find my feminine energy. It also helped me refrain from having sex with a man who I thought was relationship material. I could wait to see if they cherished me first. I wanted to be the woman a man loved so much that he watched her every time she went in and out of a room or made efforts to sit close to her. I was too focused on the lockdown: a masculine conquest. Because I had no idea what courtship was, I went with the "he likes me and I like him so we better lock this down" approach. So I started asking feminine women lots of questions about being with men. Suddenly, I gathered a new form of confidence. I could date and learn what I liked and how I liked it. I could say "no thank you" and not lose sleep.

I was wiser about how to approach relationships with men after the abstinence. Yet, I had still gone on too many dates with men with red flags. I was so smitten about my newfound femininity that I hadn't built the next muscle of discernment, which was aligned with good values. I remember the first kiss with a guy I thought was good and safe. It felt like a drug. I wandered around my house in somewhat of a daze afterward. I became obsessed about what our kiss meant and what he thought about it, and where this relationship would go. I started to create a home with him. You know, that crazy woman thinking. Then I thought, *Shit, I'm not going down this rabbit hole again.* I created a new energetic mantra: "He is just a nice man who likes me." I said it over and over and then turned the outcome over to God. I would think, *He is just a nice man who thinks I am a sexy woman. In fact, he may think I have it all.* Yet, it wasn't my career and my sexual prowess that attracted him. It was my ability to show up and be feminine, to move slow, to communicate, and to be honest.

Feminine Leadership

Being entrepreneurial can be masculine. When I was running movie sets, I was very masculine. "Hard day won, to the bar, boys!" Now as I run my business as a book coach, I can see when I am in a feminine state of holding space for a writer's words and narrative journey, but also when I am too hard-driving and demanding when people are incapacitated by their feelings or have doubts about their worth. I understand because I am a survivor. I am a better leader and teacher when I enjoy a balance in my dialogue that doesn't need a masculine-driving directive. I can speak to the heart of what they want and need versus just outcome.

Early in recovery, an uncomfortable masculine feeling crept in while I was working at my desk. I felt a hardness in my energy. I was now radically self-aware of the masculine trauma energy trying to seep back in. I took a break and rode my bike to an AA spirituality meeting. It was not a coincidence that I was the only woman in the group of about fifteen men. God is funny. He showed me that I can be vulnerable and feminine around men. This meeting was healing because I shared openly about the masculine energy that overpowers me. I didn't want it, and I wanted to be free of it. The men heard me, and I felt a layer of unnecessary masculine energy leave. None of them wanted sex from me, and I wasn't impressing anyone. After that day, I never felt that pervading masculine energy again. While I sometimes feel big like a guy in my body, I am more feminine than ever. The irony is that feminine intuitive energy actually keeps me safer than masculine energy because it draws people to me who are aligned with my soul energy. When I am in the masculine state, I attract unhealthy, power-hungry people because my heart is not centered as a mother, an intuitive, and a coach in that moment.

ENERGY MANTRAS FOR SURVIVORS

As you discover where you are depleted in your feminine or masculine energy, you get to practice new behaviors that shine light onto your neglected half. People will notice a change in your outlook on life, and you will be able to cultivate longer-lasting relationships. You will no longer be afraid of the self you will reveal, and you won't always be exiting stage left from intimacy. When I began to soften into less control over everyone and everything, I found I could lean into more of my feminine flow.

No matter how long you have been living without an identity, you're not going to ease into an absolute authentic feminine grace at the snap of a finger. You won't suddenly know how to balance your energies, but if you understand what drives you to hide in your masculine energy for protection, or to be subservient in your female energy, a new vision of yourself will grow. What used to be painful, isolated survival eventually becomes genuine living.

As a single parent, I am the head of a household with two kids, and many sides of old masculine energy try to emerge and take over. Usually, they are motivated by financial or emotional fear. I have to remind myself that allowing my feminine side to thrive does not make me weak but rather gives me unlimited strength. We need to continue to give kudos to both our masculine and feminine energies because they are our yin and yang. We are a whole person, not divided halves. I can enjoy pretty things while also love power tools. I can allow myself to be emotional at the drop of a hat but in a gentle, nurturing way. I also know when to zip up the feelings to be attentive or responsible to the task at hand.

Balancing out the feminine and masculine energy requires daily work and a powerful level of awareness. If you are recovering from sexual abuse denial, you may have subconscious loops in your head that have kept all parts of yourself protected and separate for survival. You have compartmentalized yourself. Mantras are an excellent way to cultivate a balance of feminine and masculine.

Here are some energy mantras that you can use in your daily life:

Romance and dating

"I am safe and smart about my choices."

"I deserve to be courted and cherished."

"Love finds me where I am and serves me well."

Work stress

"Everything works out in my favor."

"I can have endless abundance and joy."

"I am being called to the vocation of my whole inspired self."

Parenting

"I hold deep, loving space for my children."

"My children look to me for safety and guidance."

Finances

"Everything I want and need is coming to me in abundant amounts."

"I can achieve financial wellness without overworking or overachieving."

Today, I am on the path of a woman who loves her femininity because that was my depleted energy source. Occasionally, my femininity is profoundly awkward, but when my feminine energy is balanced, my days feel glorious, vulnerable, and empowering.

You will know when you are on the path of energetic alignment from your abuse denial, and you will feel lighter and free of self-judgment on your new journey to a recovered energy. When you find new rough edges, you can hunker down and do some more work. The good news? You will never feel less than you felt before.

THOUGHT-PROVOKING QUESTIONS

What is the most dominant energy in you currently? Masculine or feminine? What role do those energies play in your life?

Where would you like to better explore your feminine or masculine side?

What comes to mind when you think of "intuition"? Do you think it is a worthy concept, or are you immediately dismissive?

What is your definition of how you feel energy in your body? What would happen if you surrendered your life quest to fight the body that was violated and allow it to flower and open?

Chapter 11

THE INNER CHILD

We all have an inner child. The inner child of a survivor, especially one who comes from denial and repression of abuse, is unresolved and still fighting to be seen and heard. An inner child can be defined as the "repressed memories and feelings from your childhood that resurface from time to time,"[15] but I would like to take it a step further. I have worked with healers who have taken me on meditative explorations of the trapped feelings of my younger years, and I have seen the actual young me at various ages wrapped in cobwebs and hidden in dark caves. This visual—my subconscious manifesting in a physical form—encouraged me to finally show my young inner self the love and consideration she had been denied for so long. I had to look her right in the face, and what I saw was a dirty, abandoned feral child staring back at me.

Prior to uncovering the abuse, my inner child was not part of my concern. Ever. I was resistant and judgmental of the people who spoke about taking care of their inner child. Big eye roll to the folks who had actually done this woo-woo work. I had enough trouble tackling maturity as an adult in the real world with two children, never mind adding an inner child with demons to wrestle.

As a child, I was taught that I had few needs. I was used. I was a vessel for pleasure, and my ultimate value as a child was to

---

15 Sarah Jeanne Browne, "5 Self-Soothing Tips to Heal Your Inner Child," *Forbes*, September 2, 2021, https://www.forbes.com/sites/womensmedia/2021/09/02/5-self-soothing-tips-to-heal-your-inner-child/.

comfort and support a man who was supposed to be protecting me. As an adult in abuse denial, disassociating with men was a favorite ploy of my inner child because she was never given an innocent childhood. My inner child was searching for the answers to the questions: Who are men? Why do I like them and fear them at the same time? All my inner child remembered was my dad's gentle touching and how conflicting it was. For a long time, my adult self struggled to be touched in that way. Slow sex was painful and frightening. I eventually had to tell my inner child that I could handle learning about men in a different way than my dad taught me. I needed to be present. I can breathe into slow intimacy and explore a reclaimed body.

When I first started abuse recovery, I did not understand that I had to spend time healing the child within. My inner child was sitting on a stool in the corner covered in sticky chocolate, a soiled dress, her plump arms defiantly crossed over her chest, refusing to set me free until I listened to her and heard her voice. Instead, I pushed any validation of her away and projected her rough rawness onto all kinds of people so I could keep them emotionally at bay with my anger. *I'll piss on you before you piss on me.* I had no idea how to ask for what I needed, and no one taught me when I was young what to ask for. I was a pissed-off, neglected kid trapped in an adult woman's body who didn't even know what it was like to be a woman.

In recovery meetings, women would talk about their dirty shame. Because of the abuse, they couldn't feel their own bodies and would scream relentlessly at their children and their partners. They had terrible tantrums at work. The louder they screamed, the fewer people heard them and the more damage they did to themselves and others. I was a raging dramatic screamer. *You will never find the real me in here because I am a lost little girl,* I would think. I would tell my ex-husband I hated him. I would call him an asshole and a dickhead. Growing up, my dad used to call me an asshole. While the words stung, it was his lack of remorse or apology that caused the most damage. Parents are human. We have breaking points. I would never ever call my kids assholes, but there have been moments when I have gone off on critical tangents. Then I make amends afterward without blaming them. "Mommy shouldn't have said those things and she is sorry." Children are incredibly forgiving.

PERSONALITY SURVEY

Your screaming won't stop until you address the little person inside of you who is screaming to get out. When I started to release the shame of my abuse secret about a year into sobriety, I softened and realized I wasn't as angry as I thought I was. I was actually a nice person. People truly liked me. The unmet needs of the inner little girl who was angry and felt abandoned no longer ruled the adult me.

One time, my Al-Anon sponsor, who was also a friend and fellow creative, suggested that I write to five people I had recently worked with and ask them a few questions about what they perceived to be my strongest assets. Family members and friends would be too familiar and might have a more biased perspective. I was in tears as my work colleagues described me as "friendly" and "the good guy," "got stuff done without being a tyrant," "compassionate," and "likable." I saw that I was changing. I was aligning with a core underdeveloped person deep underneath. My perception of myself was so radically different from what others observed in me. I saw a dark, loathsome inner me. People saw a lovely, hardworking woman with a fun spirit.

Now it's your turn. Ask five people who have worked with you recently in some capacity to fill out a short questionnaire about your personality.

Here are some questions you can ask:

1. What are my strongest assets?

2. What has been most memorable about working with me?

3. When did they notice when I was compassionate?

4. What did they learn about me in our time together?

Absorb what their perception is of you and ask yourself why you can't see the positive attributes that they see in you.

GOD'S ROLE IN FINDING MY INNER CHILD

At the start of my recovery, one of the most painful pieces was witnessing my inner child's anger at God. My male provider's selfish hands marred my child self under the watchful eyes of God. *Where was God? He did this*, I thought. My childhood image of God was a man, so it was very hard to separate him from the acts of abuse. As I understand, my abuse ended between the ages of eight and ten, and during that time, the once-curious little girl developed a persona of an inner child who would use cunning, manipulative, angry, sexual, and violent behaviors to keep out God. She didn't have a spiritual chance. My inner child had been turned into an evil, incestuous participant. She was convinced that she would always be a little monster who wanted to harm herself and the people she loved, then hate herself for it, because no one would ever hear her, including God.

I had to grab my inner child at some point and tell her, "Look, we can love ourselves. The madness can't go on. We are going to love ourselves if it is all we can do for a while. God loves us."

I finally realized that God did not do the abuse to me—a human did—and that human had lost their spiritual path. I realized that God had actually saved me from any worse harm. God knew I would go on in life as a warrior, find my voice, and write this book to help people who didn't know how to get through their pain. I sobbed a lot while opening up my inner child to fun and whimsy. I told her it was okay to remember the bad monsters spawned by evil—they have no God, but I have God. Now I see that my message is one I can share with other men and women who feel robbed of their childhoods and the natural inner-child progression. We get to look into what we love to do without judgment and what can still be childlike even in our adult state.

Today, I belong to a Southern Baptist church because I love the hour of singing and prayer before the service, and there are other survivors in the community who also attend the church. When I am there, I realize that God has always been with me, holding me. I had found my inner child through many spiritual paths, including meditation and breathwork, but I was eventually able to bring back to my life the church that I had loved attending with my grandparents. Not the Catholic Church of their era, but the church that worked for me and my whole inner self. Getting onto the spiritual path first is key before you can reclaim the inner child relationship.

INTUITION AND THE INNER CHILD

When my dad died in 2006, I felt an intuitive urge to find clarity. I had no clue about what. At the time, I decided to get off Effexor, a medication that treats low-grade depression and anxiety. I had been on it for ten years and stopped taking it because I no longer had anxiety. I wanted to feel all the aspects of my dad's death and not be numbed by a pill. When I was off Effexor, I was more awake, but I was also raw. Without therapy or God, I didn't know what I wanted to feel about my father's death. There was a vague, nagging feeling that I was supposed to find clarity about *something*. I had no idea it was a panic because the perpetrator had died, taking my secret with him. My inner self fought to not let the dark secret die with him, yet I couldn't claw my way to the truth.

I was not yet in a position to trust my intuition, which was telling me it was time to face the truth, let go of denial, and be set free. I was running on will, not intuition, and that will had powered my life up to that point. As messy and tangled as my life had been, I was still alive, and that was my baseline as a survivor in denial. The will to live was stronger than the ability to be present to my intuitive self. My inner child had willed her way through the muck of disassociation and breaches of trust, and she wanted me to live.

As I've said before, we can't blame ourselves for how long it takes to finally face our abuse. There will be many baby steps in your search of clarity. You should never look back with regret and say, "I should've known then and dealt with it, and maybe I would still be married, or I wouldn't have become such a drinker, or I wouldn't have been rough on my kids because I have no love in my heart yet." We are not to blame. There is no manual for survivors to find their intuitive inner selves.

I can't stress enough the value of therapy, support, and community if you even feel there is a possibility you were abused. If you crack open the door of knowledge and possibility, your intuition will show you the way into the depths of what you need to know. Our path is exactly what it is supposed to be. Even the coping skills I developed throughout a lifetime of denial have become assets today—assets of courage, strength, and empowerment. When we are talking about chasing bigger dreams post-discovery of abuse, no time has been wasted to get there.

Intuition is a new gift that allows you to step away from being ruled by your inner child. It replaces that young, angry repressed voice with one that wants you to be on a safe, prosperous spiritual path. Trusting your intuition is not to be taken lightly, especially when it comes to what I have coined the "Shiny Object Theory." People like quick solutions to their problems or instant fun. Small children like shiny objects. I don't need to go toward shiny objects for solutions. I have discernment and intuition.

Finding your intuition is a process of learning how to share, and even overshare, with others. You get to have dreams and reignite what you are passionate about in your whole integrated self. While you may hold back and still not trust in some areas, the more you lean on your intuition, the more it will guide you where you spend your time and energy. You may have an impulse to do something that feels out of left field. Trust it! Long, dormant parts of you are turning back on. Lean into it. When you listen to your intuition, you will be the light that illuminates the path for others.

My inner child finally trusted the adult me, but it took years after facing the wreckage of abuse, getting sober, recovering from achalasia, falling in and out of love, and then finally surrendering to the fact that I didn't know at all who I was. Developing an intuitive muscle gave me insight into the real me.

INNER CHILD MOVEMENT

On behalf of all survivors, I am calling for the Inner Child Movement. We have to know how she has been operating all these years so she can authentically live her life free of sexual abuse denial. To understand our true selves, we all need a connection to our younger self. Our inner child exists from the moment we are born, but we are the most impressionable between the ages of one to five. "Children's brains develop connections faster in the first five years than at any other time in their lives. This is the time when the foundations for learning, health, and behavior throughout life are laid down."[16] Therefore, if that inner child faced abuse, her original self was stripped of its innocence and harmed.

I was asked to lead a writing workshop at a women's AA retreat, and I discussed the inner child without knowing how many of the women had been abused. I knew many of us drank to cope with our low self-worth and trauma. Based on my own dreams when I was eight years old and what I heard from the other women in the group, I estimated that the ages of six to eight represented our inner child's last sense of hope before she closed off and shut down. This is a time when we would have thought our dreams were foolish, either through conditioning or self-sabotage.

I created an exercise for the women to write about who they wanted to be when they were eight and what had happened to that dream. When the women shared their writings, the general consensus was shock and sadness at what they had abandoned in themselves, because what was once an innocent and burdenless possibility had become heavy due to self-repression for survival in adulthood.

I used to think that all of my big, loud, messy emotions were the result of losing my mind, but now I realize that voice was a little girl who was never heard. Knowing this allows me to control the energy and direct it toward productive endeavors. Connecting with our inner child will help us become better friends, parents, writers, entrepreneurs, and workers. We can start to feel comfortable in our adult skin.

It's time to live and to play without regret.

---

[16] "Child development: the first five years," Raising Children, accessed July 2, 2022, https://raisingchildren.net.au/newborns/development/understanding -development/development-first-five-years.

YOUR DREAMS AT EIGHT

Now it's your turn to join the Inner Child Movement. I encourage you to write your answers in a journal.

- Who or what did you dream of being when you were eight years old? If you wanted to be a stand-up comic, why did you stop pursuing that dream?

- Create a timeline of when you stopped not only pursuing the dream (if at all), but also when you stopped using those skills or aspects of your personality.

- If your dream at the age of eight feels unrealistic today, what can you do in your current environment to excel in your gifts and talents?

- How are you using those skills, talents, and gifts in a different context today?

THOUGHT-PROVOKING QUESTIONS

Describe what your current inner child would look like. How would your inner child be feeling?

When was the last time you engaged in a childlike activity, like going to an amusement park or building a sandcastle? What is your version of innocent fun?

What was a time when you acted on your intuition or inner knowing? How did that situation play out?

Chapter 12

SURVIVOR POWER

For the burden of recovering from abuse, you are granted an extraordinary gift to take the world by storm through the resilience you build in your healing. While you may feel like a puddle of emotional goo on many days, this shedding of your sexual abuse denial and reconciling with your true self creates a powerful force. That does not mean survivors universally launch their new self-empowerment into the world in one fell swoop. Everyone has their own timing and pace. We gain inner power to assert ourselves into our new life path when we are ready.

How do you know when it's time to step out into the world as your new self and feeling powerful? Ask yourself these probing questions:

- Are you moving beyond the label of "survivor" to give yourself permission to live your life to a new level of power and courage?

- Are you defining your recovery from abuse as an act of strength versus a painful slog?

- Are you able to courageously say you are an abuse survivor without feeling like it is a detriment in your life?

In your survivor power, you get to live empowered by your courageous ascent from the abuse and live your life on a less fearful level. I was in my forties when the denial was released from my subconscious, so I wanted to make up for lost time! It was my responsibility to launch my healing and stand in the new realization that I had the power to live an incredible life.

I have a deep appreciation for the rich experiences that unfold on a daily basis with my kids and friends, as well as my book coaching business, writing books, and sobriety. I am a thriving abuse survivor. I loathed myself for so long that it is a profound experience when I get to be a student of self-love. I can taste the value of it with deep gratitude.

Healing takes time, but at a certain point, the magic of your success comes into the equation, and that is a new "problem" to cope with. Getting the life we have always wanted but could never access from deep in our heart is actually hard! Especially while also attempting to learn to love. If you came to terms with abuse in your twenties and are now in your forties, you will have experienced a different recovery path because the pain has been spread out over a longer time period. You could have also swept it under the carpet and remained disconnected until now, realizing that confronting your truth is the ultimate gateway to your power. Some people are just done with accepting what happened to them decades ago and choose not to make their past a part of their present. After I emailed my mom about the abuse, I called my friend for support. Her long-term clarity about her own abuse helped me move forward from the repressed pain and shameful secrets into a more magnificent decade of life and beyond.

HOW TO GAIN YOUR SURVIVOR POWER

Little identity shifts began to occur about three years into my recovery. I was not aware that these shifts in perspective were going to lead me to an even bigger shift in perspective in the coming year. Now, eight years into my recovery from sexual abuse, I have gained a new level of power through a deeper emotional self-regulation. Instead of being triggered by fear of abandonment or loss of trust, I rely on the tools and knowledge I've learned that will help me feel emotionally free and empowered.

In the sections that follow, I discuss the most direct inroads to building your survivor power.

BEING IN AWE OF NATURE

Part of empowerment as an abuse survivor is the relationship with nature. There are psychological benefits to finding awe in nature. "Experiences that arouse awe can help us to reconceptualize our sense of self, our role in society, and from a more cosmic perspective, our place in the universe."[17] We need to be able to show our system that we can cultivate intimacy in what we observe through our own sense and imagination, especially after the disassociation that occurs when being abused. We are realigning our body and mind through a new lens that is in reality, which allows us to be less concerned with the self-preservation that denial incites.

The splendor of fully living in our new selves in the beautiful, wondrous world can bring us to pause at double rainbows blessing the sky and the endless variety of flowers in a simple garden. We have weathered emotional storms, and now we can be present to the suddenness of a lightning storm or gales of wind that whistle and rattle the windows of our homes. Trees are a powerful part of nature—rooted, grounded, and formidable. I have always found solace even just standing beneath a tree.

I always felt a melancholy sadness in fall weather. It brought up loneliness, separation, and a disconnection with my body. Rain, in particular, made me feel messy and scattered. I was not able to embrace the beauty of the changing seasons. To be fully

---

[17] Emma Stone, "The Emerging Science of Awe and Its Benefits," *Psychology Today*, April 27, 2017, https://www.psychologytoday.com/us/blog/understanding-awe/201704/the-emerging-science-awe-and-its-benefits.

present on our earth, connecting with the seasons and the moon, says that you are willing to explore a relationship with your spirit that was once trapped by abuse memories. Rainstorms now excite me, and I can embrace weather variation. Instead of inclement weather being trouble, it is celebratory. I look at rain as a unique gift.

Survivors don't love unpredictability. Many survivors want control over their circumstances so they know nothing bad will happen. Weather and nature can be spontaneous and expansive, and it can also trigger memories. While dusk in autumn can still bring up a sense of fear (the words that whisper in my head, *I don't want to go home*), I can face that fear and ask God to help me to embrace the colors of the "magic hour" that I love as a visual person. The brightness of the evening at seven o'clock after the springtime change brings me hope for a new dawning of a perception of weather. As a conscious survivor, I am witness to a range of reactions and feelings to nature, not just dread that there was some kind of climate change that affected me adversely. For the first time, I feel like I am a part of this earth again as a whole human.

As a child I escaped into nature. In the fields surrounding my house, there were six-foot-tall grasses that I could hide in. I would ride my bike down to the ocean and just hang out. I spent a lot of time with my aunt's golden retriever. She was a dear friend. I remember burying my face in her golden fur, voiceless, looking for answers to a simple "why?" She provided an innocent safety. I imagine I was hoping to escape my secret world by bonding with a harmless creature that gave me unconditional love.

I took two beautiful trips early on in my recovery so I could be more connected with nature. I went to the Esalen Institute in Big Sur, California. I volunteered in the gardens. I hacked at fennel until my back ached and pulled weeds from lettuces with burning thighs. The seals on a nearby rock barked incessantly all day. For my service, I was given access to the salt baths where men and women congregated naked. Shy at first, once I lay in the warm, bubbling baths with other naked strangers, I saw freedom from shame. I spent the night in the New Camaldoli monastery in my own little hermitage up on the highest point in the Big Sur area and woke in the morning to literally be over the clouds that covered the Pacific Ocean. My second trip that summer was to Idyllwild, a gorgeous mountain town about an hour outside of Los Angeles, where I stayed in a small cabin with a hammock. When I wasn't procuring food from the local supermarket or hiking in the vast silence, I spent most of the day in the hammock. I read an entire book. I was with myself in nature in the most profound way.

After these experiences, I started to ask myself: "What do I really want for myself on this earth?" I hadn't ever really wondered beyond what I thought I was supposed to want: marriage, children, and winning an Academy Award.

We can often discount the nature that surrounds us even in an urban environment. When was the last time you went for a walk and really looked at each flower or noticed a hummingbird? How about watching the leaves dance in trees? Take a walk wherever you are and see where you can find awe in nature. You will be surprised how much you miss when you are not looking.

LEARNING YOUR VALUES

One day it hit me like an arrow pinging a brass bowl sitting on my head. What are my core values? I was beginning to take ownership of this life that I could now see as my own, and naturally when we are ready to go deeper, teachers appear. People were talking about values with me and asking me what I valued. At first, I thought it was just another exercise to put more pressure on getting my life together, but then I realized how vague and dismissive my values were.

Values are what makes us fulfilled and happy to wake up every day. We can shape what we want to do with our time every day based on what lights us up. We can avoid people, places, and things that do not align with the goals we create through our values in life.

Now I was challenging myself to think about what I, as a grown woman, was willing to attract into my life and stand by no matter what. Understanding your values helps you to narrow down what you love and believe in.

Here are a few examples of values:

education	creativity
service to others	personal growth
spirituality	marriage
financial independence	community
parenting	nature and vacation
physical and emotional sobriety	home and aesthetics

Years into my sexual abuse recovery, I discovered how much I loved to acknowledge the homeless person on the corner with a dollar and some apples from my tree instead of looking away because I didn't think I could possibly have a solution. I loved being the soccer mom who organized the game snacks schedule. I picked up the drums again. I discovered how much I valued homeownership as a woman and started taking actionable steps to buy my own land. The value of marriage and long-term partnership emerged despite being divorced twice. I was able to reevaluate how quickly I got sexually intimate with someone, knowing I first needed to see if they could be a partner. I would have never had any of this clarity on my values if I was still in the darkness about my abuse or hadn't spent the time each week in therapy. I saw a doorway to more change and a second chance to shape my life with new values.

If you can live your life according to your true values as a newly healed person and want to attract a wonderful partner, you will find others who share your values and standards. Don't doubt. I doubted in my seven relationships (I dated a lot in recovery!), but I healed a little bit more with each relationship and was able to explore versions of being loved.

As a personal growth exercise, take note of your values. Write them down, but don't edit yourself. There is power in discovering what values resonate with who you are today. As your recovery from sexual abuse evolves, revisit the list, which will evolve over time. You get to marvel as you watch yourself change and become more vigilant about using your values as your guideposts.

POSITIVE SELF-TALK AND SELF-LOVE

How do you talk to yourself on a daily basis? Do you look in the mirror every morning and say, "I love you"? If not, don't worry because most people don't! We may do loving mirror reflections for a little while and then forget. The next thing we know, we are beating ourselves up for forgetting a meeting ("You are so stupid, you should have set an alarm!") or not speaking up when we knew we should ("You are too scared, you will never get what you want."). These hard, damaging voices come from an inner self-loathing caused by the shame we felt for holding our denial inside.

When I realized that I had power over my mind and body through positive talk and self-love, I also could stay in places of belief and not listen to a mind that was seeking danger.

"Am I okay with who I am today?" Some days, answering that question isn't easy because I am constantly changing as I heal from the abuse. I need to always be okay with who I am now.

"Man's rejection is God's protection" was a phrase I heard in recovery that gave me great hope. Think about when you hold on too tight to the outcome of a business deal or a relationship. Can you feel free and light about the situation and believe all of life's beautiful gifts will come to you? When we are in recovery and not denial, we get to make choices on how we see our lives turning out, and some of the best medicine is believing in the positive.

Early in my recovery, I hired a life coach. I was not loving the bad voice in my head. My life coach taught me that the voice in my head was a saboteur and says things like, "Who do you think you are to dream like that?" or, "Trite little fool, hapless dreamer." She taught me how to communicate with the saboteur, or in other words, "Tell the little fucker to take a hike." She showed me how to step out beyond survival and say to the Universe, "I'm going to blossom." She taught me about survivor power and the "wow" factor. When I quieted the self-defeating voices, I was blown away by so many aspects of life, such as the light in the trees, a writing class, my children's laughter, the ocean, reading a great book, or writing at my desk. I was given a new beginning and it was wonderful.

Then she asked me, "What is it going to take for you to just be okay with everything you are doing?" I didn't know the answer at the time, but I know now: love yourself unconditionally and don't strive for perfection. I was blinded a bit by frustration of how long it took to get better, but I simply got better under good direction over time. I didn't need to strive for perfection by any means. When I am perfect, I am actually dead. I had been beating myself up my whole life. I was exhausted.

I also know that when my mind is racing with a story I am

spinning, I have arguments with people who are not even present. In these arguments, I predict outcomes so I feel like I have control. Some people wear a rubber band around their wrist to snap when their head spins with toxic thoughts. Other people exercise. I like to listen to any affirmation talk I can find on YouTube during a walk. After ten minutes, I can't even believe the nature of my suspicions and judgments just hours before. They seem insane!

It's easier than you think to speak to yourself with love. When you wake up in the morning, say to yourself, "I love you." When you go to bed at night, tell yourself that you did a great job today and that you love yourself. Whenever negative thoughts creep in and try to convince you to retreat from your power and hide, remind yourself that you have the right to a big, full life of self-love. When I am scared to shine, I tell myself, "Nothing holds me back," as many times as I can until I believe it. Create your own mantra and give it a try!

ALONE TIME

We don't have to dread being alone. There is nothing wrong with you if you are alone on a Saturday night. You have a lot more ways to have fun at your fingertips than you give yourself credit for. We have a whole life to explore, free from the bondage of our abuse repression, and time is ticking! When I was complaining about having nothing to do, someone told me, "Boring people get bored." So I got busy really fast!

You can go to the movies or a concert by yourself if your friends are unavailable. How great is it to choose your own seat right smack in the middle of the theater and eat your own popcorn? Look for opportunities to be around people in this beautiful world that is full of so many fascinating activities, sounds, and colors.

I found that I like to be with me. I have funny observations, and I like to talk to strangers. I did not get sober and face abuse to spend every weekend alone on the couch like I did when I smoked pot, used alcohol, or was in my unhappy marriage. I can balance being alone with a bath, a book, or a good show, and also go on adventures. Slowly, in its own time, I let my new life and my connection to my Higher Power help me make a course correction. I also learned that I don't need to fix everything that troubles me right away. There is a good chance that the negative brain is looking for something wrong when there isn't one. I'm used to being on high alert; I got good at it when I would listen for the abuse coming. I don't have to deal with being on high alert in the same way anymore.

For example, one weekend I decided to not go out to a party and instead stay home in the rain. I made myself a healthy dinner and read a Victorian novel someone had suggested. My brain tried to tell me I was a spinster home alone with the cat. (I know you introverts think this is a wonderful evening, but I am an extrovert through and through!) I gave myself permission to ignore my mind and simply enjoy comfort with myself. Honoring myself gives me strength and power for when the time comes to go after my dreams. I have a full life that needs downtime in order for my values to manifest.

I understand that the word *alone* can have negative connotations. I would say the only negativity is if you are isolating to your detriment. In recovery, we learn to listen to the parts of ourselves that know and want what is best for us. You can begin to be at peace with your oneness without being lonely. I am glad I had that glorious chance to lay on the couch with a book because life got super busy again and I didn't get another chance for months. So don't doubt experiences! You never know when you will not have them again when your life gets hectic.

BREAK THE NUCLEAR MOLD

Another subtle change in building my power as a survivor occurred when I agreed to believe that it was okay for my current family to consist of just my kids and me. I usually dated men to find the right person to complete our family, but I was flying under the radar of my standards. A family needs a fourth person, right? I had never hung up pictures of myself with the girls. I resisted by justifying to myself that it would be too expensive to enlarge and frame the photos. But the real question that was scratching my brain was, "Who hangs pictures on the wall of just three people"? Then the day came when I realized I was doing myself and my girls a disservice by not being confident in our family nucleus. My omission created falsity. So I hung a photo of the three of us and another photo of the two of them above the TV. I had lived a very tumultuous life under an untold secret, and now I could do anything dynamic! Even though putting up a photo may seem like an easy thing for someone else to do, it was a big victory for me.

Part of sexual abuse recovery is identifying the lingering feelings that we are different from others and therefore alone. The circle you surround yourself with is your own unique tribe, and whether you are a single parent, a large family, or part of a community, take pride in leaning in and being part of the herd. It will move your recovery forward.

A NEW VIEW OF TIME

When you come into your power as a survivor, you begin to develop a new relationship with time. You are not filling every second to avoid facing abuse. When I started to honor time to let my life unfold rather than controlling every second of it, my life was filled with more unexpected wonders and an expansion of life experiences. Time expanded as I willed myself to look at it positively. The abuse took time away from you not just in the acts themselves, but also during the years of mourning. Now you don't have to rush. The demons won't get you anymore. You have earned the right to start living.

Our desire to show love and kindness grows, and it takes time to get there. I set aside small spaces of time—ten minutes here and there—to build on an idea, record an epiphany, or call someone to ask a question. These pieces may seem inconsequential in terms of time investment, but they are far more valuable than the hours I would force myself to "learn" something or "drive an idea to fruition." My life projects have come together with an unimaginable ease. I now understand how to use time as a component of happiness.

Can you imagine this for yourself? How does it feel to believe you have all the time to create, love, feel, and breathe? It's okay if you are not there yet. These changes come slowly, but when they occur, it is powerful. You get that eyes-wide-open benefit to say "wow" because it is so radically different from the time perspective of abuse.

With the magic of healing, I can shine as brightly as I want on any given day. It is limitless. In my new power of my realized self, I can see small miracles of wonder and delight, and enjoy my fellow people in the world. I understand that life is not a race to the end. The poison is out of my body. I am no longer the angry tiger with the thorn in her paw. I am a bright white dove in the sky. I can soar and be a full human. I am not halved or punctured anymore. Yet, the battle scars remind me every day to be so much more than my little mind believes. The miracles occur all around me. I don't want to miss a single one of them.

THOUGHT-PROVOKING QUESTIONS

Do you see new life experiences unfolding around you?

How do seasons affect you? What season creates joy, and what season causes feelings of loss or fear?

What were some of your experiences in nature you had as a child? As an adult, can you now be in nature alone? What does that feel like?

What changes can you make to your environment that reflect your new values? Do you feel proud of the family you have built?

What areas of your life do you believe you don't have enough time for, or where would you like to devote more time?

Chapter 13

EMERGING FROM SHAME

When was the last time you went an entire day without feeling shame? As sexual abuse survivors, we are raw and vulnerable to a variety of emotions and ailments. According to Saprea, a nonprofit organization dedicated to helping children and survivors of sexual abuse, feeling shame can have an impact on your sense of self, emotional health, and physical health, to name a few. We were shamed when we were little, and then we carry that shame into adulthood and shame others. But you can change your relationship around shame and how it makes you feel. "Due to your brain's incredible capacity to adapt, rewire, and form new neural pathways, you can reroute thoughts of shame and self-loathing (no matter how deeply ingrained or long-lasting) toward thoughts of self-worthiness and self-compassion."[18]

Shame was the gateway emotion that led to all the addictive and destructive coping behaviors, which kept me living my life in denial about my sexual abuse. The word "shame" can be defined in many ways, such as the guilt you feel when you do something wrong or some other impropriety. Yet, as a survivor, when I stare down shame, I feel that I am in some way rejecting a part of myself that makes me less whole. I carry this baggage with me, and the more I lug it around, the more I believe I caused it in

---

[18] "The Effects of Child Sexual Abuse: Shame and Child Sexual Abuse," Saprea, accessed August 21, 2022, https://youniquefoundation.org/resources-for-child-sexual-abuse-survivors/effects-of-child-sexual-abuse/shame-and-child-sexual-abuse/.

some way. I fall into a cycle of believing I am a bad person, and as a result, I act in shameful ways. The shame keeps building on itself.

I reached a point in my recovery where I was so tired of beating myself up for acting out of fear because of shame. Shame causes us to blame people in our lives. We become suspicious of their motives, suspecting that they are out to get us. Shame prevents me from living in the present because I'm afraid of what others will do to me. You can keep a healthy and protective gauge with others, but the people who have earned your trust are not out to get you. They are not igniting your shame with their actions. The negative voices in my mind want to accuse the people I love of some wrongdoing, but that is the shame of my past creeping up.

Today, if I feel I have done something that could require an apology or correction, I accept responsibility immediately, but I don't feel ashamed about my actions. I see them as information from which to grow. I don't even dabble in remorse because it also opens the door for shame. I used to blame and point the finger at others. *You did this to me; you did that to me.* I berated lovely people and walked away from friendships. I was a victim. Obviously, that was not the path to enlightenment!

Do you ever wonder why you are so concerned about others' actions? What happened to you as a child negatively affected you. You may never be fully free of the consequences of the abuse, but you can heal by breaking the trauma cycle of fear, reaction, and then shame.

FACING YOUR SHAME

The fear of being wrong in our thoughts and actions brings on shame. You can sabotage your success and land in shame if you are afraid that you won't be enough or that you will fail. Shame separates us from others and keeps us at war with our heart-led intuitive selves. You will feel ashamed for not going after a job promotion because you fear you won't be good enough to succeed. We have negative patterns of detrimental behavior that keep us in the shame loop and not in our most joyful selves. If you feel shameful about something, fear is truly rearing its ugly head.

Survivors of sexual abuse experience psychological effects that are detrimental to their emotional well-being. Many survivors hold on to a lot of fear because their world was violated and didn't feel safe. Those feelings of stress and fear then follow us into every area of adulthood—relationships, career, marriage— and we're left to somehow deal with a myriad of things. You are in fear of intimacy, so you don't show up for your partner, and they get tired of it and leave. You feel shame for letting a good relationship die.

When my emotional net widened and I saw life from a less combative place, I became more accepting of other people's behaviors that used to drive me crazy. I used to have angry outbursts at intrusive noises that would lead to day-killing shame later. When my ten-year-old daughter sang loudly in the bathtub, or my six-year-old daughter stubbornly cried when she didn't get her way, I used to feel invaded by their sounds. When I started to understand that the world wasn't an assault on me and I didn't need to live in silence to be safe, I began to enjoy expressions of sound around me. I wasn't having angry outbursts (except for occasional complaints about our cat's guttural call to the neighborhood feral cats). I was able to be around other people who express themselves because I had a voice of expression as well. I was breaking free from my bond of shame, and I had more empathy and room in my heart for others.

It is not easy to face our fears and shame. But if we start looking at fear and shame as intertwined, we can disrupt the patterns before they even start. This takes time and practice. Facing lifelong fears, or even newer fears, must come from a place of love and gentleness.

SHAME TRIGGERS

Every person's experience with shame is unique. What can be more complicated to navigate is shame that is triggered by events that haven't even occurred (premeditated fears). You may start worrying about what someone might say or do before the altercation even happens (if it ever does at all). You see yourself being violent, reactive, or retaliatory, or maybe the voices in your head scorn you for not taking action. For example, your neighbor is parking too close to your driveway, and you are afraid they may react adversely if you approach them, so you shy away from taking care of yourself. You also worry that if they react negatively, you may yell and call them names, and then you'll feel ashamed for being out of control.

Think about the actions you've taken over the last few months. What solutions could exist if you were not operating from a place of shame? You could pray or meditate on the answers, as well as consider new approaches.

Look at the parking scenario again. Instead of getting mad at your neighbor, you can approach the same scenario from a calm mindset. You could say something like, "You are parking too close to my driveway and I don't like it." Or you can suggest an alternative that will benefit everyone: "I know parking is really challenging in our neighborhood, but I almost hit your car whenever I back out, and I would hate to damage it when I am rushing to work."

It is important to realize there are many alternatives to the outcome of every scenario.

They rarely ever look like what is in our head. We can stop

living in black-and-white thinking or fearing the outcomes will not be in our favor. When our actions become more stable, we will have less to apologize for or regret. Our world is in the process of turning around and providing us what we want and need.

I want you to take a deep dive into your shame triggers. If we discover the root fear of the trigger, we can begin to unlearn shameful reactions and spend less time in a negative tailspin. Remember, our goal is to shed the layers of denial, which include old thinking and behaviors

In the following exercise, identify one to three fears that can trigger shame, and then take contrary action in the conflict.

1. Identify an action that caused you shame.

   Example: "I yelled at my daughter because she didn't clean her room."

2. Describe in one sentence what fear your actions were driven by.

   Example: "I am a bad parent for not teaching my daughter how to clean her room, and if she doesn't clean her room, things will get out of control."

3. Describe why you feel ashamed.

   Example: "I have been trying so hard not to be a yeller and I blew it. Now I feel so bad that I yelled at my daughter, so I retreat from her in shame."

4. Write down the same scenario with a different outcome.

   Example: "My daughter didn't clean her room, and instead of yelling at her, I counted to ten."

What helped me was shifting my thought process about fear and shame. I didn't want it to rule my life anymore. Don't get me wrong: our fears and shame are legitimate! But in order to heal, we need to approach our fears and shame in a new, fresh way.

FREEDOM FROM SHAME

How wonderful would it feel to live your life free of shame? If that sounds impossible, read the tips below that I used to work through my shame. There are many feelings and emotions that can aid in personal development. You could feel disappointed or embarrassed, but these states of being have more tools of communication to help you overcome a negative mindset. When you are disappointed, you can acknowledge why and look at your expectations. When you are embarrassed, you can learn to share with others and discover they barely thought twice about what happened.

Shame, though, is a whole other beast. When we stew in shame, we can't learn more about who we are and what motivates us in our lives. We are unable to build a self-awareness that is non-judgmental. You may discover you are a sensitive person, and that may never change. You get to learn to teach people how to speak to you and offer feedback in a way you can hear it knowing you are sensitive. But you don't have to hide and lose your power of self in shame.

Stop Running

If you are running from your past, you are abandoning your ability to face yourself and heal, and you stay in a shame cycle. You need to stop running from fears that bring on shame. Generations can be saved by stopping the psychological patterns of abuse and the shame.

I was always a runner to avoid the repercussions of blame. When I was younger, I would run away from my dad and mom when they chased me because I had mouthed off. They would corner me under the bed, or my dad would chase me around the kitchen table. I was scared. I became a long-distance runner when my second marriage was failing. All through that marriage,

I ran from the moments I didn't like with a powerful conviction and rage. I would storm off from volatile arguments and into the streets of London, San Francisco, Berkeley, and Los Angeles, often drunk, with no money, and in high heels. Sound familiar? *You don't love me so you don't get my love, and I will prove it by testing you to your limits. You are wasting my life away.* That high state of anxiety for so many years was what finally bottomed me out. My addictions were just seepage from the portals in me that had been sliced open from a lack of self-care and continual shame. An IV of shame. I smacked into brick walls all the time, running and looking over my shoulder to see if shame was going to catch me.

When my eldest daughter was nine, she became a runner like me because I was unable to give her space for her emotions before I was in recovery. She was in my way when I wanted to get buzzed or stoned on the couch at night and she wouldn't go to bed. As she got older and I got healthier, she realized she could run away from any conflict with rage. She had the power to hit me. She could start to revolt against all that repression. She blamed me for the shame she felt.

As I healed and continued to emotionally support her, I was granted a miracle. She stopped running. It happened while I was helping her with math. My dad had a short temper when he helped me with math, so I never asked and would fail tests. So I made a pact with myself that I would keep up with my kids' schoolwork, especially math! At first, our math sessions began with me calmly explaining the work, and then my daughter would go off the rails, shaking in the corner, yelling that she would never understand the work. I felt incredibly helpless. Then she would tell me to leave her alone, and I would think, *She can't do this alone. She doesn't need to do this alone.* But I was powerless. All I could do was love her as she was.

But then one day everything changed. We were working on fractions, and as I started to explain the math problem, my daughter was escalating into "I don't understand" mode. Then I saw her flinch. Her whole body wanted to run . . . but she stayed.

"Wow, you stayed. You stuck it out," I said.

The look on her face said she understood exactly what I meant. She didn't want to run from a conversation with me or her difficulties. She wanted my help, and by staying, she told me that she trusted me and trusted that I wouldn't be volatile, mean, and run from her either. She had witnessed my new healthy behavior for some time, and she was willing to bet on the fact that she no longer needed to escape from pain anymore, but rather there was the presence of love and understanding. It was a freeing moment from shame for both of us. I was able to help her at ten. No one helped me at ten, but I could reverse the pattern of my family's history. This was a parallel universe that two women of different generations were walking through. I was convinced she would always be a runner. I had prayed to God about it. But everything chaned that day.

Replacing Shame

We are human, so we are going to make mistakes when coping when other people let us down. As I mentioned earlier in the chapter, when we replace shame, we get to explore a new host of feelings. If we made a behavioral choice that didn't pan out in our favor, we can either be sad or regretful, or we can show some compassion to ourselves for trying our best. We don't have to immediately associate an outcome with a fear of being judged. We also get to try again next time and have a journey with our mess. The saying "The miracle is in the mess" is so true because I have acted out of fear many times and then felt a tinge of shame about how others reacted. Yet, at the end of the day, I learned so much from my efforts and from the outcomes. How can we grow if we don't show up? You get to replace shame with "I tried" or "I did my best." If you are honest with yourself and you didn't do your best, you can look at what held you back and work with concrete solutions. Shame is not a solution.

Seeing the Shame of Others

When I was a substitute teacher during my recovery, a boy in my class was always knocking his colored pencils all over the floor. It was very distracting to his work.

"Why don't you get a pencil case?" I asked him.

He shrugged. "My mom won't buy me one."

What could I say to that? In Culver City, shocking poverty exists in the homes of some of these kids. I saw a shadow of his shame. I understood because I was reconciling mine.

That night I thought about the mugs on my porch someone had given me as planters. They had cities on them. I took the Tokyo mug and plopped it onto the student's desk the next day.

"For your pencils," I said. "And I don't want to see you being distracted from your work with them again." I felt pretty good about my kindness, and he was clearly pleased with the gift. I showed love to a stranger. I could have doubted whether I was enough to show up like that with a mug, but I didn't. I operated from the heart without shame. I was a good person.

Here's the best part of the story. A year later, no longer a substitute teacher, I picked up my daughter from school and saw the boy. He pointed at me and said, "You were the teacher who gave me the Tokyo mug for my pencils."

I nodded.

He smiled. "I still have it."

That was a win of wins. Satisfaction and warmth spread over my whole body. A grin involuntarily took to my face. I allowed myself to feel good because helping others when they are in shame meant I was moving away from mine. I knew I wanted to do kind acts like that again. I moved further away from the old, abused mental state of blame and shame with every good act that affirmed I was a good and worthy person. I wasn't a piece of crap who just got lucky with some happiness from time to time.

I also stopped seeing other people's shame as a weakness. For a long time, to avoid my own shame, I was hard on myself and others. When you stop shaming yourself and love yourself, you have more compassion for others. They are no longer a mirror of your own shame. As your life grows more consciously precious, you won't choose to squander days on this earth in shame. Not everyone is in the same healing timeline as you, but little acts of kindness can boost another person up. If you detect shame, that is because you have been so close to it personally. Now you get to give back.

Celebrating You

We squash our shame when we celebrate ourselves. You get caught up in the joy of acknowledging your gifts. I know that can be one of the hardest concepts to swallow. The old you did not celebrate or celebrated a bit too much (another vodka shot, please!). The old me ran from any emotions that would require trust. We have gone the hard way of life to not celebrate our whole selves. We carry around a thick, hard shell on our bodies until it is no longer possible to avoid a self-celebration.

When I got sober, I had to learn when to pat myself on the back and say, "Good job. That's enough for today." For someone who was yearning to be seen, heard, and understood, I was not comfortable with the spotlight on me in any way, yet at the same time I was dying for attention.

I had a party in my new intentions for my forty-sixth

birthday. There wasn't a band or unlimited shrimp cocktail. It was in my small, comfy apartment. I had close to twenty women come over potluck-style and trim my artificial Christmas tree with the ornaments I had collected throughout my childhood and adulthood. The experience was warm and safe. As people ate, sang karaoke, and put ornaments on the tree, it was not all just for me. I had created a space for many women of different backgrounds and personalities to come together and commune on a Sunday afternoon. I thanked my kids when I blew out the candles. They had tirelessly helped me throw the party. Something shifted for them that day too. They saw a full mom, a happy woman who was finally wholehearted and clear when she said, "I want to play."

I thought nailing this "celebration concept" could take a long time, especially if I had to keep creating the celebrations. It was so foreign to me. It was always risky. *I'm tired. I don't have time to create reasons to celebrate.* We talk about waiting for the other shoe to drop in twelve-steps. For me, it was the Universe's big, fat, meaty hand squashing me right in the middle of a happy squeal. I didn't think I would ever get a second chance because of my past shame, not accomplishing enough, partying too hard, cheating on men, or my lack of compassion for my children.

I felt like the walls would tumble down if I showed too much cocky joy to "the life camera." These reactions are entangled with a lack of trust and a hesitance to surrender. The solution is befriending the middle ground rather than only seeing the highs and lows of experiences. I never thought I would be calm, thoughtful, and intuitive. Yet, the celebrations come in the most profound and gratifying ways with simple planning and foresight from my intuition.

The progress is knowing that the celebrations *are* coming and can take you far away from shame. The Universe can gift you with exactly what you need and deserve. You don't have to feel shame if you say, "That was a real win, Universe. Thank you." Celebrating you isn't just birthdays or holidays—it could be as simple as relaxing on the beach on a Sunday for a week well done. The process of celebration can take on a deeper dimension in your life.

Here is the big secret: once you start celebrating yourself, whether it's discovering your love of going to baseball games or rock concerts, you'll want more. You open the door to a voracious desire to make up for lost time. Plus, you start to really narrow down how you specifically want to celebrate. While I was in awe that I could throw a party at my small apartment, when I turned fifty, I got a junior suite on the seventieth floor at the Intercontinental in Los Angeles, which has floor-to-ceiling windows and 360-degree spectacular views of the city. While this was a splurge (including having my hair and makeup done for the big night), I was still in touch with my frugal self. I made cupcakes and invited a few friends to the room to eat them, and when others joined us, we celebrated in the hotel lounge, which was free if I ordered some appetizers for the guests. I could be in luxury without having to ring up a big tab on my credit card bill. While my forty-six-year-old me woke up on my couch, the fifty-year-old me was stretched out like a starfish on a king-sized bed! I recall thinking several times, *Who is this woman I have become?* I felt no shame for knowing what I liked.

Are you finding it difficult to move the needle toward celebrating yourself? What about celebrating other people's successes? How much fun is it to be around people who are reaching for their best in life? Think about who you could champion tomorrow and practice celebrating them. This can neutralize the process for you and trains your mind to think, *This is just what we do . . . we celebrate!* When you get better, you will discover the solutions to live because you have been a smart and crafty survivor. Now you get to use these gifts for others.

We can free ourselves from shame and fear, and thus blaming others, by understanding our core self, our values, and accepting our life day by day in its celebrations and wins. We can also build trust with others by admitting our moments of shame. Sharing the secrets takes the power out of them, and we can see through the eyes of others that we weren't so bad after all.

THOUGHT-PROVOKING QUESTIONS

What makes you feel shame every day? Start to notice when you feel ashamed. Are you allowing others to send you down a shame spiral? Or are you the culprit of your own shame?

Has your family changed their behavior as you grew less volatile and ashamed?

Do you still blame yourself for your actions toward others while you were in the throes of sexual abuse denial? What would it feel like to be free of that burden?

What is your most shameful secret? Write it down, then tell it to someone you trust. Then set it free.

Where in your life, and with whom, do you feel the most comfortable sharing new parts of yourself? Where do you still hold back from celebrating and why?

What are some of your recent wins that are worth cele-brating? Are they little acts of faith or unexpected gifts given or received, either tangible or verbal? Honor them even if you feel shame for celebrating yourself.

Chapter 14

DENIAL MEMORIES

Once we face our abuse memories, returning to them is not high on our list, nor do I think we should be forced to relive painful experiences. While remembering our abuse is sometimes necessary for recovery, we can also become slaves to our memories if they hold us in the dark past. Abuse survivors can hold themselves hostage to recurring trauma from the past. Survivors may not even notice because the triggers are very covert, and they still believe they are unworthy of living in better circumstances. We react and then label ourselves "overreactive," and pray these uncomfortable nagging signs go away. These unnecessary holds to the past return in recovery until they are addressed. However, once you address them and start to see new progress in your recovered life, it is important not to fall back to trauma-blaming yourself or justifying current behaviors because of the recurrence of memories. If your life is getting better, roll with that new path. What needs to be processed will continue to appear as lessons or signs. Once you are out of denial and the floodgates are open, events will force you to face the truths of what happened to you. When we come out of sexual abuse denial, we now operate with a deeper awareness of self-love and confidence so the insistent feelings can't be ignored, and we make new choices.

I am a firm believer that our stuff also holds the energy of our old memories, especially those that are more recent, such as behaviors and coping mechanisms that stemmed from denial. The abuse memories themselves may have been a few isolated incidents, but because we have been operating as a false self, we have created shameful memories in apartments, on couches, in bedrooms, around workspaces, and in cities. Atmospheres, items, specific articles of clothing, pictures, and furniture can hold us in shame and remind us of our questionable behaviors. Not only do we need to confront our past, but we need to let go of the stuff that can trigger painful memories.

STUFF OF THE PAST

One of my attachments to the past manifested itself in an old couch that I had in my possession when I was going through abuse recovery. Having a couch for over a decade may not be an issue for some people, but it was a painful trigger for me. It was a reminder of coming home day after day and sitting on the same couch that held the energy of twelve years of drinking and smoking pot, having sex with a disconnected heart, and fighting and brooding with a simmering rage. Sure, there were sweet memories. When my oldest daughter was two, she would hide behind the big couch cushions with her friends. It was adorable, but I was so far removed from joy and burdened by a heaviness in my heart at the time. I had bought the couch because it was really big and provided lots of space for me to disappear and hide. I realize now how much I wanted to put barriers between myself and other people when the biggest barriers were actually inside of myself.

I had brought the couch, with all its stagnating memories from my past, into my new apartment where I was now divorced, a single mom, and sober. My reasoning was practicality, but the truth is, the moment I realized something was very wrong about still owning that couch, I should have acted on it. Instead, I loathed the couch for another three years. I hadn't yet realized that the troubling memories outweighed the good ones. At the time, I was working as a substitute teacher and couldn't possibly think about entertaining the cost of a new couch despite having thousands of dollars in my savings account. In 2015, as I started to gain confidence as a book coach with my business and healing as a survivor, I had a shift in thinking about money and abundance. I still didn't know when my next client would sign on, or how the bills would get paid every month, but every time I saw that couch in my apartment, I would feel ugly, dirty, and shameful. Its existence no longer aligned with my new positive thought pattern. I remained trapped in the past by the patterns of denial that were associated with that couch. It was also dirty from use, and I had given up on dry cleaning it, so I told my kids to take off all their school clothes before they came near the couch. "Don't dirty the couch," became my afterschool mantra. This is ironic because that couch was filthier spiritually than they could ever make it. That was when I knew I had to let it go.

I expressed this feeling to a dear friend Gale, who is a money intuit and a former book client. I was in a session reaping the benefit of her insights. She was amazing at what she did, and I knew she would have some clarity about the couch.

"I hate the couch," I confessed to her one day. "It makes me feel poor and sad and saggy every time I walk into the room and see it. When my kids are at their dad's, I don't even want to sit on the couch and watch a movie. I mean, I want to be alone and watch a movie, just not on that couch."

"Get rid of it immediately," she said. "Give it to someone who will love the couch as much as you hate it. And send me a text when it's gone."

Telling her this truth allowed me to let go of the couch that reminded me of my sicker self of the past. We can be prisoners to our secrets, and this was a big, shameful one. So I advertised the couch on Craigslist, and a couple bought it the same day. I even threw in the coffee table. They had no furniture and were building a life. They would have no baggage with my couch. They could be free to do whatever was in their destiny on that couch. I hope the couch brought them the hope that it gave me when I let it go.

When I gave away that couch, I gave away memories from a mind numbed by alcohol or weed and the desperate need to be loved. I gave away all the fights with my ex-husband, and all the times he or I slept on the couch because we hated each other and had no idea how to pull ourselves out of the dark hole. Every time I had sex on the couch, I had to clean it as if I was a bad dog. And that was exactly how I felt: like a bad dog. I was so desperate to have sex and validate my worth—I was an object to be penetrated. Afterward, I would clean the cushions and place them everywhere to dry. It was exhausting and mentally taxing and not even worth it. But I would be satisfied too. *Look what I did. Good dog. Wag your tail. Good dog.* I can't believe I am writing this, but as abuse survivors, we have to be honest and open about our bodies. I have the words. My reaction to being pleasured is not a dirty thing. Having a healthy desire for sex is normal.

When I finally got rid of the couch, my dark thoughts told me, *You are impetuous and crazy.* Isn't it funny that I had that thought about the freedom of getting a new couch? A year later, that same voice returned when I booked tickets to take my daughters to Spain, but I had built up a muscle of resistance to it. I had learned from that couch, and we happily went to Spain.

When you remove old objects and stuff that holds the energy of the person you once were, you can now fill the hole that remains with who you truly have become in your recovery. You will make some new discoveries about your style and taste.

Marie Kondo built an empire by showing people how to clear

out anything that doesn't bring them joy. You can do the same for your healing and well-being.

THE NEW BLUE COUCH

There was an empty space in the apartment when I got rid of the couch. A new hole I created needed to be filled. What kind of couch would the new me buy? The abundance of possibilities morphed into panic. What do I love? I was stuck in my limited experiences. I knew buying big stuff in the past felt forced and unaligned. I understood God was with me in every area of my life, and I would have to wait for divine guidance on the couch. What scared me the most about buying my first adult piece of furniture alone and sober was the message to the Universe that I was ready to build the home for the life of the *real me*. I no longer wanted to be the false me who had lived under the lies and devastation of the abuse. I deserved to surround myself with beauty in my apartment no matter how uncomfortable it made me feel.

The kids and I continued to "camp" in the living room, and I prayed for what I wanted to reveal itself in the most natural way. The vision you have of your whole life is reflected by your surroundings, and so I was taking this first step seriously.

Then one day I knew. I wanted a blue velvet couch. Gaudy? Tacky? Hell no! Awesome!

My friend Jeff made me the couch. A year prior, I had stapled swatches in his warehouse for $10 an hour to pay for Christmas presents for the kids. Now he was making me a couch. It was incredible. Instead of panicking as I wrote the check for the couch, I trusted in my newfound maturity that money comes and goes, and the money spent on this couch would be replenished.

When I sat on my new blue couch and surveyed the rest of the apartment, everything else was so depressingly brown. How on earth did I accumulate so much mahogany furniture? Nothing had color. I had been living externally what I had felt on the inside: like shit.

Now I was evolving into a woman who wanted more color and vibrancy in her life. I was willing to go find it. I had to quell the desire to change everything right then and there. The fun is in the journey, not the destination. One needs to have the awareness, then acceptance, then take action, which is often easy when it is guided by God. I etched in my mind a road map to de-mahogany my place.

Clearing the couch was the impetus for my new direction of thinking. Our old stuff that holds shame or ties to old patterns or paradigms keeps us from envisioning a new future. Our trauma keeps us buried by false behaviors and identities instead of allowing us to be the person we have always been under the surface. When we let go, we get to be loud and fun or quiet and contemplative. We learn to bird-watch and collect origami. We start to hope for more connection with others rather than feeling like a facade of ourselves repelling the world. Our yearnings can be difficult to understand. I cried when I discovered for the first time that I really liked a particular color, texture, sound, or saying. I discovered I liked leather pants and seventeenth-century French portrait art. We gain a new life and a deeper intimacy for ourselves.

Soon after I bought the couch, I got tired of my daughters arguing about sharing a room. To keep my sanity, I gave up my bedroom to split them up, and I started sleeping on the new blue couch. This time was quite humbling. Every morning I would take off the sheets and put the big pillows back, and every night I would "make my couch." Sleeping on the new couch for two years stopped me from having parties because I didn't want people to ask where I slept. However, it did push me out of my comfort zone. When I booted the old couch, it opened the door to progress and started a new trajectory of my life.

We may not see the progress right away. Even though my brain tried to play tricks on me while I slept on the couch, I knew that if we had moved to a three-bedroom apartment, I would never save up enough money for a house. I had my eye on the prize of homeownership, and I fought off the negative thoughts that said I was "pathetic" for sleeping on a couch. As I made more money and had a new vision for my home, the apartment that had been a safe space to start recovery from sexual abuse started to deconstruct. Its time had come. The pipes groaned and clanged whenever the shower was turned on, and the bathtub simply stopped draining and Drano didn't even cause a threat. I had grown weary of looking out the kitchen window onto a parking lot and pretending as if it was my beautiful ocean or sprawling yard view. We had spent six years yelling at our cat that desperately tried to escape whenever the door was open a crack, and the only place for him to go was under greasy cars because we did not have our own outdoor space. I wanted our cat to have a yard. I prayed to God to show me the path to buying a house. I accepted that I needed to be in a state of forgiveness and gratitude for this apartment to finally let go. I felt like I had outgrown it, but I was terrified of moving into a house *alone*. Didn't I need a partner first?

Then my friend Gale said, "I don't care if you are not ready to buy a house yet. You have to get off the fucking couch."

She showed me where to put up a screen to turn the dining room into a bedroom, and we moved the kitchen table to divide the apartment into three little areas. Then I had to buy a real freaking mattress. This started my journey of sleeping behind the screen, but it still had no privacy. How do you "go behind a screen" on your kids? The area was right next to the kitchen and off the living room, so it was just the next leap to consider moving. The cat was in the living room all the time (thank God I went to an office to work or I would have killed the cat). I couldn't spend another minute sleeping behind a screen, but the truth was that I was once again growing up and moving toward a less memory-fueled future.

We are creating memories all the time, so as we recover from the abuse and the denial, we make smarter choices about who we want to spend our time with, how we spend our money, and who we share our sexual intimacy with. I was conscious about who I allowed to come into my house to sit on my couch and sleep on that mattress. I was afraid of making more bad memories. I dated gentle, kind people and stayed away from any kind of real trauma. I wanted to move with that couch and mattress one day, free of conflicts and negative energy.

When we move forward in our cycle of becoming the true identity of who we are and are no longer suffocated by the trauma of the past that can keep us stuck, each step represents a new level of strength and courage. We get to own the memories we make in our work and home environments. Shedding memories and behaviors of our past abuse gives us the potential to create meaningful snapshots in our new life. We have the bandwidth and the awareness. What we see for ourselves in our future and the ability to reach for bigger dreams is linked to how we adjust our space.

ENVIRONMENT SCAN

Now it is your turn to take an honest assessment of where you live. The energy in the environment where you spend a lot of your time should be supportive of a new outlook. Material possessions can trigger old feelings, and you want your environment to be safe and joyful all the time, especially when you are in recovery.

- Scan your environment. Are there any objects that hold negative memories or reminders of your behavior in the years of abuse denial?

- Make a list of every object that holds a negative memory or reminder of the past. For example, the glass in the corner of a picture frame is cracked from when you threw something at it because you were angry. Don't dismiss any object that has a negative reminder, whether it's a piece of furniture, a memento, an article of clothing, or a photograph.

- What are the pros and cons of keeping this item?

  Pro: The object still serves a primary purpose, and to replace it may not be financially sound at the moment.

  Con: You are reminded of old emotions, such as low self-worth or frustration, every time you see the object.

- If you decide to keep the object because you don't have a replacement, you are at least aware of the emotions associated with it. Start to look at how you can logistically move forward to replace the object. I got rid of my couch, which had caused many negative emotions and grief, and I went without a couch until I finally found one that brought me joy.

If you notice there are more negative objects, you are blocking the energy of your recovery by remaining in the past where you operated out of denial behaviors. Your goal is to surround yourself with only things that will illuminate recovery and the new you.

THOUGHT-PROVOKING QUESTIONS

What objects from your past with bad energy are you holding on to that you can get rid of today?

What type of judgment are you afraid you will face if you throw something from your past away?

Look at your surroundings and honestly ask yourself what makes you unhappy. What is holding you back from expressing aesthetics that you may prefer? What would it feel like to embrace new desires or interests? Is it liberating or confusing?

Chapter 15
COMMITMENTS

Clearing out old clutter that was connected to my old thinking and operating patterns was revealing. I realized I was lacking the commitment to identify new values, dreams, and desires. Asking "Who am I?" is so cliché, but after denying who you are for so long in keeping the secret self at bay, you now have to commit to the new person you are becoming. You can live with one foot in and one foot out of commitments while justifying it to anyone who will listen as "exploring my options." But that doesn't produce million-dollar results or lifelong marriages, especially when life has been harmed by a spiritually decrepit panic or fight-or-flight mindset.

At this time in recovery from your denial, I can't stress enough how important it is for you to commit to, without wavering, learning your new values. If you understand what is valuable in your life, you can then commit to obligations and life assignments. Keep your eyes open because God, your Higher Power, your spirit guide, or whatever you believe in, is showing you the new path. You must follow the path even if you are unsure where it leads.

Joining AA in 2014 was my first real commitment to life aside from parenting and facing sexual abuse. Committing to sexual abuse recovery alongside sobriety was a whole ball of string to untangle, but once I had clarity in my denial of alcoholism and my abuse, I was able to see why I was elusive with long-term commitments in my life. Remember when I said I would run away? That was a trauma response.

Growing up, I was forced into commitments I didn't choose.

Sexual abuse was the glaring one, but I was also forced to publicly perform on the piano and attend an all-girls' school where I was bullied and unhappy. I was forced to stick to circumstances I didn't want, and I was also taught that people cut you off when they are done with you. As an adult, I made commitments haphazardly out of desperation and fear, only to find myself in misery years later, awkwardly cutting out and running. It wasn't until I was in recovery from sexual abuse and sober that I had to take a long, hard look at how I avoided commitment. I simply didn't know how to make commitment for me.

When you come from abuse, choices were made for you that were not in your best interests. You grew up making decisions that were not authentic to who you are. You made commitments to people who represent a lack of safety or elicit feelings of drama or shame. The abuse wired us that way, and while we may have gotten tangled with people who don't have our best interests at heart, we can commit to making better choices for ourselves today. The key is learning to listen to our body and heart more than our mind. Turning the tide and giving to others on your own terms is a practice in humility.

BUILDING TRUST THROUGH COMMITMENT

Part of not committing is the learned belief that we are different from others because we have been abused and are damaged goods. We can take it too far and believe we will not be included and liked. Then that old comparison card comes out and we think, *These people are not like me*. This mindset is from a lifetime of stuffing down feelings from abuse. We dodge situations that could benefit and expand our lives because deep down we don't trust that we are doing the right thing, or that we will get hurt if we stick around. But survivors are strong because of what we have endured. We have a fighter mentality. We sometimes forget that part of our arsenal.

In 2016, I joined a business group of women, and the lifetime membership cost $450, plus $50 every month to attend the lunch. My new book coaching business was a year into its start, and after signing a few clients right away, I was in a slump. I needed to network to get more leads, and I was pissy about the time I had to spend to do it. Every month, I would leave in a negative huff after another luncheon spent with women who didn't seem to understand my business.

I called my AA sponsor. "These women are clearly not my people," I said, a bitter victim. "And now I've paid all this money for a lifetime membership." My inner critic wanted me to feel like an outsider, confused and hapless to levels of success.

"Can you give it a year?" she asked. "Then you can leave."

I knew she was right. This was an opportunity to practice patience in a commitment. I was treating the group like a romantic relationship. I go in all pie-in-the-sky, expecting you to fulfill my dreams, but at the first indication that you are not part of my illusion, I am ready to bolt out the door, write you off, and resent you for not giving me what I want and need.

I learned in AA to look for the similarities, not the differences, *and* to be of service. How could I use that philosophy with the women at the networking meeting? How could I change my expectations of commitment as a businesswoman? Could I help someone I met? I could think about their businesses so my ears would be open to referrals for them instead of what I could get out of it.

Regardless, I moved forward with the women's group with a new attitude: to be open to possibilities. As I asked the women at the networking group more questions about their businesses, I met my stylist, financial adviser, and branding coach. I assembled a tribe of trustworthy women. They were people I could trust with the new me because I had taken all those months to get to know them. My commitment to this membership expanded my support tribe. Eventually, I was elected an officer of the group, given a Member of the Month award, and in time, moved on because I had changed my networking business model. I did not leave in a huff or a tizzy, but rather organically with courtesy. I was quite pleased with myself.

Going to networking events also showed me how committed I was to trusting the changes I was making in my book coaching business. I attended Business Network International (BNI) meetings. At seven in the morning, I would stand in front of fifty strangers and give my thirty-second elevator pitch. My heart would pound out of my chest, and I wanted to die. I know lots of people are afraid of public speaking, but under all this terror was a woman who desperately needed to be seen in her new identity. My kids observed my commitment to building a business, and while I was a hot mess sometimes about how much work needed to be done to grow the company, they were proud of me. This was exemplified by my older daughter, who was eleven years old at the time, pitching my book coaching services to our new dentist. She saw how passionate I was about my work and felt other professionals should know. I had met the dentist at one of my networking circles, so she already knew what I did, but that didn't stop my daughter from making a sales pitch for me. After the dental appointment, the dentist gave me discount cards to share with friends.

"I will definitely give these out for you," I said. "Happy to help."

"Thank you," said the dentist.

"And you can make sure to refer clients to my mom," my daughter chimed in. "She's a great book coach!"

I was so proud she wanted to help promote me!

DODGING COMMITMENTS

This book is not an accountability self-help book. There are a slew of good titles out there that are intended to hold you accountable to tasks. Here, in recovery from abuse denial, we are focusing on the commitments you have been avoiding for "justifiable reasons." For example, maybe you didn't make an important decision because you kept asking other people their opinions until you were talked out of doing anything. In the past, I would poll a lot of people until I got the exact answer I was looking for, which justified my inaction. I didn't believe in myself enough to know what was the right action for me. As survivors, we need to strike that fine balance between seeking advice on a commitment and moving forward with a trust in our own knowledge.

Self-care commitments are another area where survivors fall short. Making an honest list of how you avoid commitments that are good for you is a way to break a pattern of not serving the best intentions for the new person you are becoming.

Write down your reasons (a.k.a., excuses) for each self-care commitment you avoided. Then come up with a counteraction or solution. The action doesn't have to be a direct solution that fulfills the commitment, but simply an awareness of where you may be dodging self-care. Track your excuses over time. You will start to see a pattern. All of this is part of a pattern of shame and self-sabotage, and the goal is to move through life more effectively so you can focus more on a self-love commitment to you.

Commitments	"Reasons" a.k.a. Excuses	Solution
Clean out my closet.	I should keep working on the project for my boss until it's perfect.	Clean out three items from my closet every hour.
Exercise every day.	I don't have time because I need to work and run errands.	Every hour, get up and move for five minutes.
Go to sleep earlier.	I worked hard all day, and I want to binge-watch a show.	Only watch one episode.

COMMITTING TO YOUR VALUES

I wish I could say that once I started identifying my values, I put a stake in the ground and told anyone who didn't agree with me to talk to the hand. Didn't happen. I vacillated a lot because many times I felt awkward standing my ground. The more we base our intentions on our values, the less sticky it gets, and we find that we actually can be more flexible around those values. We can see other people's points of view without feeling like our rights will be taken away. I learned gradually how to commit to my values in many different arenas.

For example, take my experience at Disney on Ice with my daughters. I had been in recovery, sobriety, and business ownership for a few years. I took a day off work, which was scary in itself because my income was low, but I saw the writing on the wall. My daughters were young at the time, but I reasoned it could have been the last year they would be interested in the whole princess thing. I committed to buying them pizza later, as well as the cost of the event, which led me to set up some value boundaries for any other expenditures at the event.

"I'm not buying any crappy princess toys from China. If you want a toy, you have your money with you. Also, I am not buying food at the venue. We are having pizza afterward," I told them.

Okay, I know this sounds harsh, but kids understand that money doesn't grow on trees. Please shoot me now for saying that.

The moral of the story is when I had stuck to my principles in the past to save $5 on event food, game room tickets, or (insert child expectation), I had miserable kids, and I fell into a silent fury at their lack of gratitude (or my expectations). This time, when we all got a little hungry, I bought the damn snacks. Despite my value commitment to save money, another commitment took precedence: for all of us to be happy and not hungry! Oh, you bet the old depravity rose up in me as I stood in line to buy $15 nachos and a pretzel, but I pushed through it. We all snacked on toxic crap but were happy.

The biggest victory was when my eight-year-old surveyed the toys for sale and said, "You're right, Mom. They are all crap from China, and they're not getting *my* money."

This experience taught me how to prepare us for our trip to Spain, where we would all work as a team on a daily budget for food. I stood in a deeper understanding of my commitment to eat well every day but not overspend. I did not know it at Disney, but learning about who I was in my relationship with values and committing to an evolution was preparing me to live a bigger life. Or should I say, God was preparing me.

How long have you been living on the dollars of worry and doubt? Financial fear and doubt never gets us anywhere faster or brings us any more real joy. Perhaps it is a synthetic joy, or false gratification, but it is not a pure love we can feel as whole, realized people with our children, friends, partners, community, and coworkers. You can commit to understanding why you think the way you do every day and believe that you have the right to your thoughts, but you also need the tools to understand where you may be running from commitment or placing unrealistic expectations on a life that has far bigger and better plans for you. Commit to the journey of the new you.

COMMIT TO REDUCE EMOTIONAL PAIN

If you are reading this and have children you share in custody, or if you have lost time bonding with your children due to a past of pain that you were unable to overcome until now, then commit to continuing to be the person you want to be, and the new connection with them will follow. It wasn't easy for me to make a commitment to reduce the emotional pain of missing my kids when they went to their dad's. When I started to accept myself and stopped hiding my feelings behind dead-end relationships with men, the pain of my kids leaving my home became unbearable because I had finally accessed a deep love for them. My heart was thawing out. I hurt so much when they went away. Loneliness had been replaced by genuine love. I had to fully accept that I was teaching myself how to love in a completely new way. I also had to be willing to build my new life when they were not around. In their absence, I had to continue growing so I could be a better version of myself. I was committed to a new self.

I decided to stop punishing myself for my marriage ending, which had resulted in me spending less time with my children due to shared custody. My marriage would have ended regardless of the abuse, and I needed to look at pure facts. The 50/50 custody my ex-husband and I share frees up time for me to establish new values and focus on what I want to commit to building in my life. Some nights, especially after five days of not seeing my daughters,

I want to hold them and nurture them. I feel guilty that they had to suffer through a divorce, but this way of thinking only fuels more emotional pain. The best remedy is to continue to mold a better version of myself instead of floundering in the guilt of the wreckage of abuse. The kids are loved, and they will be loved by me when they are in my home, and they are loved by their dad in his home. After all, who knows what journey my children will take after growing up in two homes with two happy parents. It may have a more positive impact on them than living with two miserable, checked-out parents who hate being married to each other.

On the weekends when my kids are at their dad's, I enjoy physical, social, and romantic activities. I commit to having fun, personal development, and self-care. I can't fritter my life away on drinking or unavailable men, or wallowing in the anxiety hole. I tap into the woman I am becoming, and when my kids are in my home, I can present myself as a strong, brave role model. They feel it.

If you are a parent, then you know what it's like to not want to get another glass of bedtime milk or are tired of playing referee to fights. Sure, it can suck taking care of two other creatures on top of yourself, especially if you are still healing. Yet, your children are part of your commitment. Healing while raising kids is challenging, but you are given a gift of reducing emotional pain by tapping into their innocent joy and accessing the child within you who needs to be healed. I have found that being with my children is an incredible gift that I had never seen before on such a deep level. My commitment has deepened beyond just their care and consideration but to my life unfolding with them in it, however that looks.

For survivors, it can be easier to love someone from a distance than to really love them, because they will not disappoint you if they act in a certain way, or if they leave you alone with these deep feelings of love. My new story is that I am a successful woman who chooses to spend the day with her children, not because she needs to. When I'm with them, I also don't waste the time worrying about my next dollar or getting lost in the fantasy of some man who isn't part of the current equation.

Commit to reducing emotional pain by first loving your new self. It will all sort out exactly as it should. Shutting down serves no one and is a waste of your body's vessel, which contains your spirit that has a divine purpose on this earth. That is not to be taken lightly. You have made a commitment now to a new existence on this earth, regardless of what has been done to you.

THOUGHT-PROVOKING QUESTIONS

What resistance came up for you while reading this chapter? Do you feel like you have special circumstances around being an abuse survivor?

What are some of your stories about overcoming limitations? Have you tracked what opportunities opened up for you to push into new areas of growth?

What part of making commitments causes you to feel unsafe or controlled? How can you feel more comfortable committing to others?

Chapter 16

CHANNELING SPIRITUALITY

After accepting the abuse and moving into the identity of a survivor, we can't stuff a new, evolving life into an old container. You may be painfully and acutely aware that the new life's working model has been like hammering a marshmallow flat, but you are unaware that a spiritual reboot is needed. If you have discounted or rejected God or any religion, entering into a spiritual partnership to walk through your new life can be a hard nut to swallow. I am not saying you should go to church or believe in God. I am suggesting that you form an alliance with a spiritual sense around you that is not the God of your childhood. I couldn't keep splashing around in a goblet of alcohol and calling that relationship God. That was a falsified, inebriated God. I had to create a new cup with God—a bigger God-sized cup that had room for all the parts of my new life to splash around in, new waterfalls of goodness to drench my cup.

Okay, enough with the cup and liquid metaphors.

I started the process to create my own God.

Call him or her your Higher Power, a sun goddess, the ocean . . . whatever resonates with you. Understand there is a power greater than yourself to whom you can turn in the depths of despair. You can say, "Help me to not feel so broken. Help me to stand tall in the face of fear. Help me to not feel so sexually frightened. Please help me to believe that I will do the right thing even if it is wrong at the moment because that is part of the spiritual path." I desired the strength of a woman who could stretch my limitations while also being vulnerable and seeking human touch and love. Discover your own prayers of hope and desire.

What all this comes down to is spirituality and where you can find that gentle shift from the "I got this handled" mentality— where it's just me, myself, and I—to a partnership with a power that loves you. Where is your spirituality? In the gentle adoration of a child's freckled nose? In a hummingbird in the flowering lime tree? In jazz music playing in the background? Spirituality and a Higher Power are found in solutions and non-endings, and a steady, even middle. God, to me, is self-love. My new God emerged with me at the pace at which I could handle the path to love. It was not mechanical or forced. Spirituality gradually appeared in everything I embraced. My Higher Power had slowly grown into someone I could trust, someone who would be there for me when I risked turning off the "monkey mind" that kept me alert to danger.

As a survivor, it was shocking to realize that in spirituality, we must actually come to terms with surrender. When I read Michael Singer's book, *The Surrender Experiment,* I was blown away by the levels of surrender he executed when life threw him curveballs that were not part of his game plan. Even when the outcome appeared grim, he leaned into divine results that were beyond his limited human capacity.[19] In my sexual abuse recovery, having a connection to God helped me set the pace for what I could handle and when I could handle it. I believed that maybe, just like Singer, I would see an outcome beyond my view of the horizon if I would only let go of the reins. God would give me a lot, or a little, and sometimes a little was perfect a lot.

---

[19] Michael A. Singer, *The Surrender Experiment: My Journey into Life's Perfection* (New York: Harmony Books, 2015).

A DIVINE CONNECTION

People who are in pain and have no outlets to heal cause other people pain. My dad has been dead for over a decade, and many new understandings of him and his emotional and physical struggles have come from simple meditation and talks with God. God helped me to shine a different light on the abuse and my abuser. God never asked me to forgive, but I saw a painful human journey that began long before me.

When I started to read the *Big Book* in AA, I found a God of my understanding. As a reader, God being intellectualized through heartfelt stories of other alcoholics in recovery provided me with my first real spiritual tribe. Some AA members define God as a "Group of Drunks." I went from rejecting the God who was present during the abuse but didn't save me, to trusting in a God who could hear my prayers maybe 75 percent of the time, regardless of how horrible people can treat each other in this world. I was willing to believe that God had been with me the entire time I was being abused and was speaking to me, but I could not hear him because I was a child. God was saying, "While it may not seem like it today or tomorrow, this experience will be part of your journey to share and help heal others someday."

Here is what I have come to believe: God does not make people do bad things; people do bad things. God just assures us that this, too, will come to pass in peace and service. You can blame God for what happened to you, but I urge you to find a new spiritual tribe to fall back on as you evolve and grow into your new body. As I grew into my new being with a spiritual partner, I was able to speak in front of groups without a pounding heart or rapid breathing. I could start to track and understand when and why the anxiety attacks occurred.

Your understanding of a new relationship with God, as well

as the bold courage to have a voice with a less prevalent sense of fear, can take time. You should not expect spirituality to evolve overnight. You can make a lifetime commitment to simply understand, but don't get caught up in an old version of God or spirituality. A weight can lift from your shoulders if you fully believe there is a cosmic spirit in the Universe who knows more about your life and purpose than you. All that is required is to show up as your best self.

When I started my journey of abuse recovery and brought God onto my team, some days we had our hands full just to keep me in the game, let alone expecting joy, compassion, and enlightenment. Over time, our work together has transformed. I wake up ready for the gifts of my life, and occasionally I need to talk to God, close advisers, and sponsors about troubles in my wake. Almost 99 percent of the time, those troubles are of my old perceptions.

As I started to communicate with God, I wrote love letters to myself and expressed my deep joy and profound sorrow. To recover from abuse, I understood that I didn't have to throw away all the parts of who I had been, but I could readdress the skills, desires, and dreams that had been harmed by a life of suffering. I needed to love myself and needed that love in return. I had to be willing to take a leap of faith that my words and writings would heal others, all because of the power of love I have for myself and others.

You don't have to believe in God or even be religious to write a love letter to yourself. Spirituality is a deeper connection to your inner self—all the parts of you that live in your mind, body, and spirit. You can have a divine connection to the love you have for yourself.

As survivors, it's so important that we learn to love ourselves— flaws and weaknesses and all. When was the last time you looked

at yourself in the mirror—and I mean *really* looked at yourself—
and gazed deep into your eyes? When was the last time you said,
"I love you," to you? It's important that we extend that love
inward. Practicing self-love can be challenging for some, but we
must look at ourselves and acknowledge everything that we've
been through.

UNDERSTANDING YOUR SPIRITUALITY

When I first faced the truth of the sexual abuse, I listened to
Deepak Chopra and Oprah's 21-Day Meditation series. I
watched interviews with Oprah on YouTube. Like millions of
people around the world, I have a tremendous respect for Oprah's
connection with her spirituality and intuition. I bought books
she suggested, such as *Discover the Power Within You* by Eric
Butterworth, and *A Course in Miracles* by Drs. Helen Schucman
and William Thetford. But what really hit home for me was an
interview Oprah did at the Stanford Graduate School of Business
on Career, Life, and Leadership in 2014. She talked about Gary
Zukav's *The Seat of the Soul* and how vital it is for a person to
change the way they think and see themselves in order to align
with a deeper potential of the soul. Oprah claimed we can learn
as much from our losses as our victories.[20]

I downloaded Gary's book on my Kindle and couldn't put it
down. As I read the chapters on intuition and the descriptions
of the soul as a separate part of personality,[21] I wondered what
had been written about sexual abuse survivors and spirituality.
I searched the internet, and a passage from Cara Stiles's article,

---

[20] Stanford Graduate School of Business, "Oprah Winfrey on Career, Life,
and Leadership," April 28, 2014, YouTube video, https://www.youtube.com/
watch?v=6DlrqeWrczs.

[21] Gary Zukav, *The Seat of the Soul: An Inspiring Vision of Humanity's Spiritual Destiny* (Rider Classics, 2022), Kindle.

"The Influence of Childhood Dissociative States from Sexual Abuse on the Adult Woman's Spiritual Development," stuck with me. According to Stiles's research, the role of spiritual experiences for survivors in their lives was a largely unaddressed area in literature. My further interpretation was that writers were hesitant to engage survivors in a discussion about a Higher Power for fear of alienating them with a potentially contentious subject.[22]

What I am exemplifying here is to do research. Get curious. Devour literature. Do your spiritual due diligence before you discount the impact of a new sense of spirituality in your life. Having a spiritual force behind your new identity can be crucial in facing the horrors that ravaged your childhood. Having a spiritual belief that you are worthy enough can carry you through the rough days and add light to the good days.

MY RELIGIOUS HISTORY

When I was a child, God was banned from being mentioned in our house after my grandfather converted from a Catholic to a born-again Christian. My wonderful relationship with this man, with whom I sang show tunes at the piano, soured almost overnight when my mother painted him as "crazy" when he remarried a woman from the church quickly after my grandmother died. I was ten years old the last time we spoke. I remember calling him one time about one of my school accomplishments.

"God did that, honey."

I was taken aback.

---

[22] Cara L. Stiles, "The Influence of Childhood Dissociative States from Sexual Abuse on the Adult Woman's Spiritual Development," *Journal of Heart Centered Therapies* 10, no. 1 (2007): https://go.gale.com/ps/i.do?p=AONE&u=-googlescholar&id=GALE%7CA162575804&v=2.1&it=r&sid=googleSchol-ar&asid=fe8002bb.

"No, Grandpa . . . I did it."

I remember not wanting to talk to him again after that because our conversations centered around God. My mom, who had left both the Bahá'í faith and her Catholic upbringing, said that my grandfather was "crazy over God." He sure sounded crazy, but I loved my grandfather. He made me laugh. He took me to piano lessons, and afterward we had turkey dinners at the local steakhouse.

But when he aligned God in this new way, I had no idea that deep down in the repression of the abuse, my inner child was thinking, *Where was God in my house full of abuse and secrets?* My young life was being twisted and warped in very conflicting ways, and my grandfather was always preaching about how God created all circumstances.

While my grandfather may have been overzealous in his Christianity, what he was saying was a truth that I would first discover in AA, where we could have a God "of our understanding." At the beginning of my journey to come to terms with sexual abuse while also writing this book, I met women who, like me, had entered twelve-step programs and were able to vocalize the sexual abuse but needed more spirituality to get them to the next stage in their lives. They needed a death of their religious past so they could renew. Twelve-step meetings—not the church or the religion of their upbringing—became that safe place to contemplate a power greater than themselves.

Women were able to put aside their religious history and deepen their connection with God in AA meetings where any religion was accepted. If they had rejected a conventional God and were living a spiritless life, they could reconnect spiritually through art, dance, nature, Buddha, or simply staying sober one day at a time. We all need spiritual healing, regardless of our religious history.

I know examining your religious past can dredge up frightening feelings because they can be linked to the shattering of childhood trust. When a small child is abused, they experience an annihilation of trust as well as their spirit. They die again and again. That is a sad thought, but as an adult, if you can transform that concept into a form of power and strength, you will be better able to understand the power of rebirth. We can use being "born again," so to speak—and I don't mean specifically as a Christian, but in your new identity—to open ourselves up to be surprised by how many miracles and synchronicities work in our current life.

You can walk out into the world and accomplish incredible things because you have seen your past, you have faced your God, or an absence of God, and you can now reshape how you want to connect to spirituality in the world.

SURRENDERING TO FAITH

Have you ever fallen onto your knees, the floor, or the sand at the beach and held yourself, but knowing you are not alone because a power greater than you is helping you through? Whether you want to admit it or not, this act of falling to our knees in reverence of something more powerful than ourselves is not just a surrender but an alignment with a new power within you.

How can survivors be asked to surrender and be powerless again when our power was once taken away from us? Isn't being powerful what we strive to achieve in our recovery? Yes and no. As human beings, we can only get so far on pure facts. We can take our life to a whole new level of depth and enjoyment if we succumb to the possibility that there is a force around us far greater than our limitations. My abuse history limited me for so long. I was ready to join forces with a spirit that could guide me into a far wider expanse of personal discovery.

About three years into sobriety and sexual abuse recovery,

despite feeling like I had found God, I realized I was still not praying on my knees. I had fallen to my knees in despair or during a panic attack, but not to purposely acknowledge a communion with God. This isn't to say God doesn't hear you unless you are on your knees, but it was a message of resistance in the inaction that needed to be addressed.

"I can't pray on my knees," I said to my friend, who had revealed he once struggled with reverence to God. "I feel like a Catholic, but I am not one."

He explained how adding that extra piece of surrender radically changed his relationship with God. I wondered if I could get down on my knees before a God who had me go through decades of abuse just so I could share my story.

I gave it a try, and when I prayed on my knees, I saw for the first time that I was praying with the emotions of a disappointed little girl. I was praying to a child's God, and that wasn't going to work for me as an adult. I realized I must create a relationship with God as an adult. Suddenly, I was liberated and felt like I had a new "God project." I wanted to show reverence to my partner in more miracles than I had seen in a lifetime. God would also be on his knees to me. I must choose to see it.

Spirit Guides

It does not take a great lightning bolt in the sky to surrender to a new faith and point of view about the scope of a bigger life. It's to see that you are deserving of a bigger life with far less pain and sorrow. With God's hand, we simply have to be willing to see the signs. Then you'll start to notice faith and a power in your existence in connections with like-minded people. I see faith and miracles through people all the time. When we are abused, our identity is not grounded in a spiritual belief system, and we can codependently cling to the wrong people, who will reenact the same dynamics we experienced in the titillation and then abandonment of the abuse. My dad would come and go at night, and I never knew when or how the abuse would happen. I grew up with apprehension and uncertainty about people's permanence. That translated into a lack of trust in my ability to discern people. As I leaned into my spirituality, I was able to avoid elusive people, create a dependency on a spiritual path, and have more faith when people showed up for me to offer opportunities, love, and friendship. They paved the spiritual path for me through their belief in a power greater than themselves. Many times, people who have not been abused and are living in the sunlight of the spirit are often attracted to me as someone they can lead and guide. They have seen my spiritual light when I thought the power had gone out for good. Overdue bill. Off the grid. They come along and see my potential and flip the switch.

To see your guides, all you have to do is to keep listening, showing up, and surrendering so you can let God lead you to the people who answer your desires and prayers. God quickly shows me new paths when I don't even know I am ready. I found a Southern Baptist Black Christian church in East Compton, California, to be my religious community. There, amid the choir song and the spirited and poignant Sunday sermons of the pastor, any unrest in my heart is soothed. I feel loved there and was even baptized. A year prior, I was skeptical of Christianity, but as long as I am not put in a box or told what I could or couldn't believe, this place has given me hope.

Allowing the Spirit to Inform

When it came to my career, I asked God what I was supposed to do for a living. Being a book coach was nowhere near my radar. That was when Jay stepped in, and seeing my light, pushed me to surrender to my faith. Jay was the speaker at an AA meeting I attended a year into my recovery. I didn't want to be there. I was in a real bad funk. It was raining, and I had no clue what I was going to do next in my life. I knew it wasn't substitute teaching. I knew it wasn't movies. I did know there was a deep ache to guide people—lots of people—and to help them transform with stories.

The secretary approached me at the meeting and asked if I could be the leader. I was baffled.

"I really have nothing illuminating to share this morning," I responded.

"No, you just read the format. We have a speaker," he said.

I agreed and stepped onto the stage and sat down next to Jay, a big-hearted man with an even bigger personality. We sat under a dangling light bulb, the glow illuminating his face. He introduced himself, and after some light chitchat, he looked me in the eyes and said, "You have what it takes to really be something. We need to turn on your light. You need to call me."

I believe God had me attend that meeting that morning for a reason, so I called the number on the card, despite my suspicions that Jay had been hitting on me. Instead, after speaking with me for an hour on the phone, Jay introduced me to women who were writing and business coaches. I did not even know this world existed. All I had ever known was movies and parenting. I listened when he said I could be a writing coach, but it wasn't easy to hear. No one ever told me those things. I chose to attend a business conference in Arizona he'd recommended. In a room with two hundred and fifty women entrepreneurs, my world was rocked and my life was forever changed. I stood up at a microphone and had a public cry with a coach and hundreds of women. They understood my confusion and desire. I called Jay during one of the breaks, sobbing.

"I think I am going to sign up for a six-month coaching program."

"That's wonderful," he said.

"But it's $5,000, and I have never invested that much money in myself before, and I am really scared." I felt like I was going to throw up. I couldn't breathe.

"I need you to take a few breaths, and then I want you to go to a quiet place and ask God what he thinks you should do. I think you already know this is something you want, and that scares you. You are worth it, Kim."

All I needed was five minutes of staring at the beautiful Arizona mountains that surrounded the Ritz Carlton, the breeze ruffling my hair. I paid in full and, shaking, rejoined the group.

"I signed up," I told the table of women where I was sitting.

"That's wonderful!" they said.

"I'm really scared," I revealed. Then the shaking started to subside because they held space for my courageous decision and told me how they had done the same, and their businesses were thriving. I was no longer alone.

My old, nonexistent God was in a bottle of wine, a cigarette, and resentment. On that day, God was present in all those women, Jay, the Arizona mountains, and me. I allowed it to be okay.

Upon returning to Los Angeles, I sat on my stoop. My street was deliciously quiet on Sundays. The wind rustled through the palm trees. I looked up at the palm fronds, the sun peeking through the breaks in a luminous shine, and noticed the browned leaves. I saw a flash of death—not my own, but the death of something within me. I felt a spiritual exhale.

As I continued to stare at the brown sticks and dry leaves, I noticed one of the branches wasn't a dried-up old plant but a brown hummingbird. The shift in nature matched my exact shift in perfection, and it had revealed my totem animal. I knew this was not a mistake. God was sending me little signs that supported my new dream. First Jay, then my leap of faith with the trip, and now this small creature shifting my perspective, beckoning. *Believe, believe.* The world may not be a dried-up old stick but rather a vibrant, busy hummingbird.

FAITH IN THE WANDERING

Maya Angelou speaks of the importance of "hours of aimless wandering." When we are children—at least my generation—we grew up watching ants and looking for four-leaf clovers. The darkness of being an adult survivor can create those voices that beat us up if we want to aimlessly wander in nature. I speak about the importance of healing in nature several times in this book, and now I connect it to finding your channels of spirituality by simply wandering in experiences and environments that bring you joy and peace. Even if the dark voices tell you that you are being lazy or unambitious with your time, you have to wander. We find ourselves and our faith in a power greater than us when we take the time to explore a new dress shop or walk into a bakery to try the samples. God is in the spaces of wandering.

"Faith without works is dead."[23] God wants to be your partner. He wants you to take action. Yet, you have to also listen to your heart. I get emotionally drained when my heart is shut down. No good manifestations can come in. When my heart closes down, I freeze and get rigid about my schedule. I direct my thinking toward surviving, not living. My crazy mind starts talking crap and I get scared, especially when it is so loud. It takes a bit to quiet it down. I can lean on God and understand I may not know the truth. The same brain that created the problems is now trying to figure out and solve the problems, and that is a losing battle.

---

[23] *Alcoholics Anonymous: The Big Book* (Alcoholics Anonymous World Services, Inc., 2002), 76.

The same brain that repressed the abuse for so long cannot be responsible for leading me back to sanity!

Where can we best practice this act of wandering to connect with our spiritual messengers, our inner intuitive knowing, or a partnership with God? As I have already stressed, you don't need to find them in a church or religious entity. Even if I belong to a church community, my God doesn't belong to any entity other than the earth and the sun and sky. My religion has evolved from none, to some, to all. Eventually, "spiritual reboots" are a key part of my schedule.

SPIRITUAL REBOOT

What is a *spiritual reboot*? A spiritual reboot is an ongoing exploration of how to channel your spirituality. It is unique to everyone. I would encourage you to make a list of activities or actions that fill you up spiritually. To help you along, I have listed mine:

- A good night's sleep after a conversation with God.

- Morning prayer is followed by an open-eye meditation practice.[24]

- Dressing nice for an event you don't want to attend. If you make a new contact or have a good time, that is a turbo reboot, but simply going can be enough.

- Asking someone about their health, job, or any current situation, and not talking about yourself at all.

- Scheduling attentive time blocks with your kids or friends when you don't look at your phone.

- Dancing free-form to music either in the house or in a venue.

---

[24] Bruce Joel Rubin, YouTube, https://www.youtube.com/c/BruceJoelRubin/videos.

- Finding gratitude in your romantic relationship or dating outside of your expectations.

- Playtime with a friend.

Some of these may seem like obvious actions, but when you are headed toward isolation or the old thinking patterns, spiritual reboots can reopen your channels to spirituality, which gives you hope for a better life. Make your list a nonnegotiable part of your "new religion." They were an essential part of my success in crafting a new life.

The core of spirituality is perspective. Surviving abuse is only one part of my story. It is not my whole story. I have so many parts to myself that can thrive and grow. The "dirty little secret" of abuse is no longer a secret but one of the realities of my past. I get clearer every day about how it affected me, but I move closer to the positive when I'm unwilling to feed into my negative perspective. I have had a powerful and amazing perception available to me my whole life, but I just didn't know how to access it.

You can find your spirituality and God in any place that works for you. Spirituality can be in the rustling of the trees and the crashing ocean. You don't have to travel to Peru or meditate for forty-five minutes to channel your spirituality. When life gets convoluted and warped, refine your religion in simplicity. Reground yourself in your spiritual reboots. For me, it is noticing the mere presence of trees. I return to my soul through their movement and sound. From there, I can bring back everything I have found intuitively through messengers of the gift of faith and share my rekindled spirituality with others who are still lost in the darkness.

THOUGHT-PROVOKING QUESTIONS

Where do you find spirituality when you need to connect?

Even if surrendering makes you uncomfortable, have you seen the benefits when you let go?

What was the God of your understanding in your childhood? Do you still look at that Higher Power, spirit, or God in the same way, or have you reworked that power?

How do you pray? Even if you don't, write your own prayer that you could say every day for the best life for you.

What prevents you from wandering? What would your ideal day of wandering look like? Write it down—the actions, the surrender—with detail and imagination, and post it on your wall. Then one day, go do it!

Chapter 17

YOUR BODY IS YOUR FRIEND

We only have one body in this lifetime. While it is true that our body has been violated and abused, it is still our body to care for and nourish in recovery. In my decades of denial, I overexercised, judged myself, marinated in alcohol, took mind-altering drugs, and took my body for granted. I had no respect for my body because it had been used to determine the worth of another in my formative years. Like many of us, I also was raised with weird messaging about my body. My value as a woman was measured by how fit I was or how good I looked. I was essentially disassociated from my body and couldn't see it as a beautiful gift that carried me through all the hopes and dreams in my life.

We now have the opportunity to change our relationship with our body. As we move into a new life of wonder and joy in recovery, we can treat our bodies right. For me, that means drinking plenty of water, eating vegetables, limiting my white sugar intake, and reducing caffeine. I am not a nutritionist, and this isn't a chapter about eating a balanced diet, but when we listen to our bodies, we hear what they want and need from us. When we were lost in the sadness and anger of abuse, our bodies were ignored. Our bodies have stood by our sides while we abused them because we didn't think we were worthy. Your body is ready for you to make the connection to your heart and soul—to fully integrate the whole you and make your body into an ally, not a foe.

To reclaim all the time lost in various states of denial, we need to make our bodies a top priority. I don't mean we have to look hot, sexy, or have the best teeth or hair. But we need to take care of our bodies and keep them healthy and strong. We can learn what works well for our bodies and also be honest about what doesn't work. I used to run fifteen miles a day when I was clueless about the abuse, but my body doesn't want to run anymore now that I have a lighter mind and a freer spirit. Now I get to love my body and do exercises that make me feel good.

I also don't binge, overeat, or vomit anymore when I am sad, lonely, or feel like I am a piece of crap. Everyone has a different timeline for healing and heals in different ways, so if you struggle with an eating disorder, know that you can get help. Food may be the final frontier to self-love, and all I can say is that my heart goes out and my hat goes off to you. Food is necessary for survival, so you must nourish yourself.

Healing our bodies is no joke, and every survivor needs to set the pace in their own recovery. What I do know is that we are all subject to a radical disrespect for the bodies that carry us. When I started to believe the "me" in this body carried a loveable, worthy woman, I became determined to protect the space where my soul and mind resided. Was it an overnight success? No! Is it still a work in progress? Hell yeah! But as I say ad nauseam in this book, awareness is the key. Simply observing how you eat, what you eat, and how you move your body without judgment is the key to making a loving change in your day-to-day love affair with your body.

FOOD AND OUR PAST

When I first started sexual abuse counseling, I begged my therapist to make sure I didn't gain weight. That was a huge fear of mine. I identified payoffs in my life with men as purely about me looking thin and good. I was never thin enough for my liking because I truly loved food and always ate. I have had relationships with food many times in my life that have been lovely, but more from an aesthetic point of view—That was a fab restaurant, or, He must love me if he takes me out to dinner. I didn't think about the food I was preparing or buying as feeding the body that houses my soul.

Food is a sense of home, and our bodies are our home. Food signals were frequently confusing in my house growing up because of the abuse and tension with my parents. On one hand, we ate natural food in the eighties with my mom, but when I moved in with my dad in my teen years, there was never any food, so I ate a lot of boiled hot dogs and hunks of Velveeta cheese. I would walk to the local Dunkin' Donuts and get a glazed donut at two in the afternoon after drinking all night. College was no better. I was so broke and would sometimes have to choose between buying ramen or tampons. Food was a scarcity for me, and I was less-than on the inside, so it made sense. When I was in situations where there was a lot of food available, I would overeat to feel like I had abundance. It didn't matter what the food was; I just wanted a lot of it.

My story is not one of a diagnosed food disorder, such as anorexia or bulimia, but I did binge and obsess over food because of the yoyo availability of food in my younger years. These behaviors can surface for abuse survivors to the point where they are distracted and checked out of their lives, their vision, and their purpose. In her book *Binge and Sprint: From Endless Cake to Recovery*, Naomi Joseph binge ate from a young age to stave off the loneliness of coming home from school every day to an empty house, but also to absorb her father's constant abusive and loud shouting. She also watched her father shove down his food and then move on to his next task. She had developed a belief that her father's coping mechanism could be hers, and her negative behaviors with food followed her to adulthood until she was an exhausted fifty-year-old. She was forced to change her inner self-love because she could no longer outrun the abusive upbringing by abusing herself with food.[25]

Studies show that sexual abuse survivors are more likely to be overweight because of the psychological component of being abused and the chase of happiness with food. I knew that being overweight would be just another excuse to loathe myself. If you have an eating disorder or are in the process of overcoming an eating disorder, my heart goes out to you as a survivor. We had our innocence taken away, and then we suffered in our coping mechanisms with food.

"Trauma that occurs during critical periods in the brain's development can change its neurobiology, making it less responsive to rewards."[26] As Joseph talks about in her book, adults with abuse history can go into a daze when they binge and not even remember what they ate.[27] So what should you do if you are in the perpetual state of crisis and using food to numb the demons of your sexual abuse?

Examining our past with food, and how we behave with what we put into our bodies with denial, is an exploratory act that can give us information about how we currently eat, exercise, or nourish ourselves. We may have patterns that won't change,

[25] Naomi Joseph, *Binge and Sprint: From Endless Cake to Recovery* (WriteLife Publishing, 2021).

[26] Olga Khazan, "The Second Assault," *The Atlantic*, December 15, 2015, https://www.theatlantic.com/health/archive/2015/12/sexual-abuse-vic-tims-obesity/420186/.

[27] *Binge and Sprint*, 2021.

but we can understand the power of messaging of food when we were being abused and after. Sometimes, I like to remember good times with food as a child, and not all memories were painful. I can also approach food without any ties to the past. The more distance you have from the initial shock of facing sexual abuse, the more you see your vision for the new you, and a lot of that is your new relationship with food and your body.

TRUSTING OUR BODY

Our relationship with our body is connected to self-love. We also have to take on some unavoidable detours to our well-being such as PMS, menstrual cycles, or how much sleep we get if we have insomnia or menopause. When I am tired or spiritually bankrupt, the low-self-worth gets played out on my body, and I fall into old patterns. Instead of taking a short power nap or praying, suddenly, "I am not enough" translates to gorging on food, particularly the self-serve bins of chocolate almonds and yogurt-covered pretzels at Ralphs. My body has shown me what I need—to rest and replenish—but I don't listen. We don't trust our bodies to speak to us.

Take constipation, as an example. It's not a very pleasant subject, but as an abuse survivor, I have struggled with trusting my digestive system to naturally flow. To do so means letting go of control. I never thought about my digestive system in a loving way, only that it needed to keep chugging along to accept all the marijuana, cigarettes, alcohol, vitriol, and rage I poured down it. How unkind I was to my insides. I used consumption to bury my sexual abuse trauma.

My body was a vessel that kept on pumping and pushing. I didn't understand what my body wanted and needed because I ignored my body's cues for so long. I was also so wrapped up in the anxious and panicked energy that I would fall back into a spiral of self-soothing that was steeped in bad habits that exacerbated the anxiety. When I started to trust that my body would flow if I listened to what it wanted, I started to explore a high-fiber diet, eat more salads, and made sure I moved my body a few times a week in a way that broke a sweat. It may sound ridiculous, but after decades of suffering constipation and yelling at my body, I now thank my body every single time I go to the bathroom.

Other people can help you tap into what works for your body through energy work. I never in a million years thought I could give up coffee. I had tried years before and got a pounding headache for days. I just didn't have the strength or willingness to persevere. I knew that caffeine and coffee were bad for my body, as I was dependent on them. I am an intuitive and an empath, so the caffeine would shock my system multiple times a day, blocking my inner voice and faith. Then one day an astrologer friend told me I should omit caffeine. I decided to listen. I went through one week of feeling incredibly sleepy, but I never got the headaches. As the dependency left my body, I realized that I was overriding my body's natural rhythms with caffeine. I trusted my body could get through so I could have a more spiritual experience with my mind on the other side. Today, I don't miss coffee, and I have a new sense of clarity. This was one of the biggest acts of self-love I had ever done for myself. I am able to listen to my soul speak from the heart and my mind because I'm not as jumpy and nervous.

Think about what changes you could make if you trusted your body. When we tap into our bodies and really pay attention, the options on how to heal ourselves are truly endless.

YOUR NUTRITIONAL FLOW

Part of changing our relationship with our body is examining how we treat it on any given day. This includes when we eat, how we eat, who we eat with, why we eat, and how we exercise. In recovery, you will want to create new patterns with how you connect to your body with food, as well as develop a friendship with your body, which carries and supports you throughout the day.

I want you to reflect on your flow with how you nourish and tend to your body for one week. We are looking to care for our bodies in a loving, connected way. This is not meant to be a food journal or a diet plan. I am not judging you on what you eat, what you can afford to eat, or when you eat. I want you to look at what you do objectively so you can see any patterns that you may want to change that reflect the old you.

If you noticed that you eat too many carbs at every meal and no vegetables, why not try to change that up? If you sit on the couch every night and think about going for a walk but instead eat ice cream, you could consider taking contrary action. When you are open to change, your body will start to speak to you. You get to have a conversation with yourself about your relationship with your body, and you'll start to notice some patterns in how you approach nourishment.

Let's look at meals as opportunities to connect with your body and what you are putting in it.

Breakfast

How do you eat breakfast? Do you jam it down in a rush while standing at the counter? Do you grab a quick donut on the ride into work? This can be our fuel to start the day, and how we give our bodies nutrition can reflect self-honoring choices in how we value ourselves. Making the first meal of the day a time to reflect in a journal or say prayers is a good way to slow down the first ingestion and allow your body to process. Coffee can also be a nice ritual. How can you change the way you eat breakfast now that you are getting to know yourself as an abuse survivor? What do you like to start the day with?

Lunch

How long does it take you to eat lunch? Do you feed yourself nourishing food, or do you rush through the fast-food drive-through? Why is that? Are you biting off more than you can chew at work so you eat through lunch at your desk? What is one scenario around food you can change during your lunchtime?

Dinner

What time do you eat dinner? Do you eat in front of the television every night? Do you eat dinner as a family? Do you like to cook? When was the last time you took yourself out to dinner?

The perfect road is never a straight line in any of this work. You are not going to change every routine in one week that has been in place in your life for months or even years. Take one mealtime—breakfast, lunch, or dinner—and make one slight change, then note how you feel. You may be surprised at how big a small change can make. Your body will thank you for your love and attention.

NOURISHING YOUR BODY

How do you nourish your body in ways that don't involve food? So many awesome ways! You can "fill up your body" with activities that are soulful, healthy, and mindful. You get to teach your body that you understand it is your partner in life, and you are having a deeper connection with it in your recovery. Here are some examples of fun ways to nourish your body:

- take a pole dancing or aerial silks class
- buy a wonderful-smelling body cream
- get some new sheets for your bed
- lie on a blanket in the park for an hour under a tree

Now it's your turn: make a list of things you can do to connect with your body. Have fun with it! Your body has been through a lot, and now it's time to honor it. As survivors of sexual abuse, our bodies were used in ways that were not natural to our emotional state. Our mind-body connection has been severed and breached, leaving us short-circuited. We now have the opportunity to deepen our relationship with ourselves. We get to explore how we emotionally feed our bodies, and then trust in them more each day.

MOVE YOUR BODY

Part of having a new friendship with your body is understanding how it moves in a way that is sensual and life-giving for you. Another part of this equation is getting the daily required allotment of exercise (thirty minutes a day) so you can have longevity in your life.

We didn't suffer this long to then come out of abuse denial and get heart disease or lose bone density. For many of us, before we faced abuse, we turned to exercise in a manic way in order to distract ourselves from the denial that was buried inside. Rachel Brooks, author of *Chasing Perfection: A Journey to Healing, Fitness, and Self-Love,* talks about one act of sexual abuse when she was a child that shattered her ability to see herself as anything other than fat and imperfect. She almost destroyed her body with weight training and body building to be as fit and thin as possible. When she faced the abuse memory and the denial, she was able to embrace a lifestyle where she could create a nutrition and exercise regimen that was healthy and enjoyable.[28]

Moving our body is an act of self-love, but it can also teach us about ourselves. I still can move at full speed throughout my day and forget to check in with my body in a loving way. Getting on the yoga mat, doing Pilates, or dancing with a video on YouTube for thirty minutes a day keeps my body strong and my mind connected.

List four ways you can move your body that is not trying to achieve an outcome except for having a connection with your body. Here are some examples:

- Walk to the coffee shop instead of driving.
- Play a favorite song and dance to it.
- Weed the garden or water the plants (if you live in a more urban area, there are lovely community gardens you can get involved in).
- If you sit at a desk all day, get up every hour and move your body for five minutes.

After you try new ways to move your body, make note of how you feel. Are you more connected to who you are and did your mood elevate? Start to note these acts of movement and make them a regular part of your week.

SUIT UP AND SHOW UP

During my first year of sobriety, I bought my first bike in over twenty years and rode it to a local AA meeting, as well as on the bike path to the beach. I remember being single and a little out

---

[28] Rachel Brooks, *Chasing Perfection: A Journey to Healing, Fitness, and Self-Love* (Ohio: Author Academy Elite, 2020).

of my mind with loneliness on the Fourth of July, so I rode on the bike path in my bikini top in the sun to the beach. I parked my bike in the sand and went for a swim in the ocean. I felt like such a powerful creature in that moment. I was using my body for fun and exploration. I did not need to do it for anyone but me. It was extremely uncomfortable at first. Now when I do these things, it's the new normal, my God-given gift. I can go to the beach and swim by myself! I'm a full human on this earth! It is healthy time with my body, not fighting fear and loneliness by abusing it.

The more you show up for the body that is yours to love and enjoy, the more you will discover a style you never knew you had. Maybe you'll want to wear different clothes in a new way, with brighter colors and styles. At my AA meetings, I took a voluntary position of service greeting people at the door. Since it was a very popular AA speaker meeting, with occasional celebrity speakers, people would dress up. I had to suit up because I was the first face people saw when they entered the building. I forced myself to clean up every Sunday and greet people. Part of serving was making sure my appearance matched who I wanted to be, regardless of my poor body image or the deformity I felt inside. I was gradually shedding my past during that time and in that service. I was not staying home in sweats. I was being visible and trying out new styles.

Sometimes the voices inside my head would say to me, *You live in lack, you aren't exercising enough, so why even try to look or feel like a healthy, successful person?* I would respond with more peace and confidence. "You are not my friend, voices," I would say, and get dressed in suitable clothes to greet people at the door to the AA meeting. Later the voices said, *You win. You are changing.*

When you discover a new sense of friendship with your body,

you now are living in the whole essence of yourself. You may be surprised by how much you can love yourself.

Someone once said to me, "If my mind didn't need my body to carry it around, it would have killed it long ago." You are working on your new thinking and vision as you recover. You will need a strong body to transport you to help others and love with a boundless capacity. You have worked on your mind, so now it is time to work on the container. You and your body are worth it!

THOUGHT-PROVOKING QUESTIONS

What were your eating habits as a child? Do you remember certain meals? Who were they with?

What are a few patterns you could change in your lifestyle that would reflect a more loving relationship with your body?

What kind of exercise did you used to do that you can't do anymore, and what have you explored as a new alternative?

What kind of misgivings do you have about the validity of your life changing if you befriended your body?

Chapter 18

SLOWING DOWN

Slowing down every day to refocus your intentions on heart-centered actions can cause panic at first. The scared and uncomfortable feelings may feel new because you are facing them without secrets. You can rely on the simple idea that everything is exactly all right just as it is. You are recovering, and your whole life as you know it will change.

I have always been a fast mover and high achiever. I get up at 5:30 a.m. and do about six hundred things a day. Not every day, but many days. My warped self-perception did not allow me to acknowledge my success, so I had to always push myself harder, and I never really tasted the essence of what I was experiencing. It was the runner mentality I had when I was in denial. I thought if I didn't keep moving, I would have to think about how there was something deep down inside I was supposed to face.

My life was all about going after grandiose high stakes and big splashes. No simple life-affirming joys allowed. Today, I am aware that when I allow space between my activities, I have epiphanies and solutions that would have been impossible to predict a year ago.

One of the biggest learning curves in my recovery has been slowing down and allowing the presence of God to speak through me. Lying still while being inappropriately caressed by a parent made it very challenging for me to be still and open as an adult. But life is beautiful when you explore all sides, fast and slow. I try to be present for every interaction, but I also don't need to understand or even clarify joy. I hear the little miracles from messengers: people in my life who guide me for a minute, an hour, or longer. If I hadn't been that abused young girl, I may have had some bandwidth to start asking, "Who am I?" Now I can, and it's not too late. It is not too late for you, no matter what age you start to face your own sexual abuse. The quality of the moments when you step into the new power of the recovered you will blow decades of your false, angry, repressed self out of the water.

When I force others to make fast decisions and solutions, I get ahead of my mind and body, and I fall back into old patterns of trauma. I doubt, panic, judge, and am overwhelmed by intense sadness. I think I am a crappy piece of shit. I punish myself. Yes, I do this sometimes even now, and as life gets bigger and more complex in all the fruitful ways, I will have many more bouts of rushing forward to manage. I can't explain why, but the slower my world gets, the faster my desires rush toward me. My life has a luscious velocity that is scintillatingly slow. What a paradox!

WAITING FOR WHEN YOU ARE READY

I lived in a perfectly nice apartment with a kitchen window that looked out onto a small parking lot. Nothing glamorous, but I could see the sunset and the moon rise. The window got dirty from the smog of the cars coming in and out of the lot, so one day I got fed up with the obstruction of my view and decided to clean it. At that time in my life, nothing was done with ease and grace, so I only did a quick evaluation of the two panes of glass, and I didn't even go outside to assess the situation. I duct-taped a sponge to the end of a mophead and jammed it between the two panes of glass. I had to get that damn window clean if my life depended on it. My kids, hearing my tone of voice and aggressive determination, steered clear of the whole operation. I was left with a six-inch clean circle and a sponge wedged between the glass panes. I rushed to a solution and had proved to myself what I already knew: I deserved only a small circle to look through because I was still a dirty girl.

Six months later, and a lot of profound abuse-recovery miles logged, I was returning from a lovely Sunday outing at the farmers' market. I had gotten used to asking myself, "What makes me happy?" On this particular morning, the voice replied, "Clean that darn window!" Within seconds, I grabbed a Swiffer wet mop and a stool and went outside to wash the window. I saw the difference in this scenario of how I approached challenges, believing that I deserved what made me happy and therefore the Universe would provide the answers. That window turned out sparkling, and for the first time since I had moved in, I could see the trees and the sky. I had not just cleaned a dirty window that day, but an old story. The only person who made it hard and impossible was the woman who believed that if she didn't do it her way, and immediately, she would never be happy. Feeling like I had to chase and capture happiness made me tense and reactive rather than simply being in the flow of life presenting solutions.

These lessons will continue to come to you on different planes of maturity. You can believe you not only deserve happiness, but you don't have to race against the clock for it. When you slow down, you can make smarter, less impulsive decisions with career, men, money, or how you react to a conflict. For those who are overachievers, this slowing-down business is a game changer. You can still be successful and not get yourself in a real mess (like a sponge jammed between two windowpanes). Slowing down forces us to sit in discomfort and trust, which build resilience toward the unknown and unexpected. While we may have mastered that state as kids to deal with the abuse, we did it in a disassociated state, not as a tool we should be passing on to ourselves as adults. Now we get to build resilience through our own self-control, timing, and actions.

TOOLS TO SLOW DOWN

- Breathe. I know I say this in a variety of ways, but the sound of breathing in and out is centering and can bring a pause to the hectic self-important hustle and bustle of life. You can try Ujjayi yoga breathing in the back of your throat, which makes a rattling noise and can distract your brain from its busy spinning. Breathing reminds us we are human beings and living on this earth under the sky, the sun, and the stars. Everything else is extra.

- Make a list of everything you did throughout the day. You may be beating yourself up for not doing enough. Your list will show you how much you actually did, and you will be more than happy to give yourself some hangout time!

- Purposely drive yourself somewhere, such as the forest or the beach, and remind yourself that if you didn't accomplish anything today other than the basics, you would not only be just fine, but you will have made the brain space to hone in on new ideas and thoughts.

- Find a support system to help you in completing tasks so that you don't reach maximum capacity in a negative way. You don't want to feel overwhelmed, as this can be damaging and lead to anger.

We can be survivors and own businesses we love, have connections with our children, enjoy romantic partners, make high incomes, and still not be stretched to our capacity. We can reach these goals by believing that happiness does not have to be hard won. When we give ourselves permission to be happy in a way that is slow, we can still enjoy a full life without overextending ourselves.

THE MYTH OF MULTITASKING

I hate to break this to you, especially if you're like me and think multitasking will get you where you hope to go, but there is no grace in juggling fourteen balls in the air, especially after overcoming sexual abuse. Why would anyone want to drive themselves crazy juggling a conference call while their nails are drying, and pasta is cooking on the stove, and they are planning camping reservations? Multitasking was how I lived my whole life until recovery. I would go on high octane and then burn out stoned on the couch. I was in extremes all the time. I never believed there was enough time to get everything done that I needed to do in life for success. Yet, I wasn't even living a true life. I was in a lie. So I did a million transitions and tasks a day, and then I struggled with the fact that I didn't seem to have any space to think or process. I knew I needed to shut off that message I had been hearing for so long: "Women are excellent multitaskers, more so than men." As a mother, I took on the multitasking role because that is what is expected, but curling my hair, making my kids' lunches, drinking coffee, and checking email all at the same time does not set my day off to a very focused start.

I began to wonder what it would be like if I took each task one at a time. Who told me I wasn't allowed? I decided to give it a try, and, ironically, I would leave the house earlier and calmer. Here is why: the more I do, the more my brain wants to do because it is addicted to being filled with stuff, which prevents me from getting to the real heart of my feelings and thoughts that will foster a connection with myself and others. When I stay in one place and tell my mind, "It is okay to be in this one place," my ego fights me. It tells me that silence is dangerous and scary. When I was being abused, my state of consciousness was to survive the silence. Now I am learning how to embrace the silence, the beauty of my soul, with my own moments in time. Sometimes those moments are shared with others. It will be a lifelong practice to listen to what makes me happy without thinking I am a loafer, a side stepper, or an addict.

The secret is that everything actually moves faster when your life is rich and full. The decisions to be in abundance and being open to possibilities are always in calm spaces. Believing in the slowness of things brings what you desire to manifest at rapid speeds. When opportunity knocks, I can say yes quickly without feeling like I am engulfing myself with unnecessary space to fill commitments. I am on this planet to be fully present in whatever I am doing and to enjoy the speed at which I set the clock.

Taking things slow won't always be easy. You will want to rebel. That is when your faith in slowing down has to be the strongest. Talk about your discomfort to people you love and trust. I confessed to a guy I was dating that I was feeling like I had to "get out" and "run" after we had spent an intense day together. I was stuck in the old thinking pattern that if there was a good buildup of intimacy, like his devoted attention, silence would disintegrate everything. I would be forgotten and left. I would disappear and no one would notice. I would be obliterated by the silence, purged of every raw essence of me, and left splayed. When I told him about how I felt, it diffused my desire to run away, and it drew us closer. I got to spend the next hour in intimacy with him instead of festering in my old programming of self-preservation. I can't go there anymore because I am no longer in denial.

My dad may have stolen my innocence from me, but my journey is to see that people simply come and go—that is the way of the natural, rational world. There is silence. As abused kids, we fold into our abuser's identity and cannot imagine having our own. We cling to the identities of our lovers, friends, and professions.

In slow action, there can be silence where all the shifts can occur. As you heal, you reconcile the adult from the child, the longing from the abuser, and slowly feel your way into your present life.

THOUGHT-PROVOKING QUESTIONS

Is it easy for you to be still and slow down? How does your mind speak to you when you take a break from "making shit happen"?

Is there a circumstance when you tried to force an outcome and had to walk away with a false belief that you didn't deserve happiness? Did you return to the scenario?

Is there an action that frustrates you and that you continue to do in defeat? If so, what would make you happy in that situation? Then let it sit until you can find a solution with a clear voice or action, and ease and flow. To help with clarity, write out what these situations are.

What is your relationship with silence? What are some words you associate with your feelings in silence?

Chapter 19
ROMANTIC LOVE

My willingness to date was pivotal to developing a healthy understanding of what partnership and "romantic love" means to me today. We all have our own definitions of romantic love, and what that encompasses is our personal ideal for commitment, sex, and intimacy. Over the years, I have noticed my patterns in romantic relationships. At first, when I fell for a man way too quickly, I misinterpreted it as a sign that my walls were coming down and I was becoming vulnerable. Yes and no. There was nothing wrong with the quick development of a relationship, but I was also impatient to be loved. I would dig for all the truths right away, but even if I didn't like what I found, I would stay longer than I should for the sex and fun, but also to complete the love lesson. Each relationship was a lesson to understand my true meaning of "the one." But what I was really searching for was learning how to love myself. While I think we all have a potential soulmate, I am learning that you still have to be intuitive about whether you are on the same level to love, and that you must love yourself first.

Even if we are struggling with what has been done to us, we are designed for human interaction. Some of my quick relationships challenged me right away by becoming too intimate too quickly because I engaged in *trauma bonding* or *love bombing*—both acts that fill an insatiable need to be engulfed by someone's affection and attention. The intensity of the love and the attraction is so hot and furious that being enveloped in the other person is almost like a high or an addiction. There's a tendency to feign an immediate closeness so there will be no fear of the unknown or being abandoned. The issue is that one person in the equation is struggling more than the other, and as a result, that person will become overwhelmed by the pace and will have to bail.

"One of the most tragic outcomes of sexual abuse and assault is the negative impact on the sense of self and how healthy relationships work."[29] So how do we find ourselves capable of having a healthy romantic relationship? Clarity comes from honest exploration that is free from judgment. When we work on our relationship with ourselves, we will align with people who are also in that space of self-love.

ROMANTIC LOVE WITH OUR ABUSER

A big ick, right? Who wants to talk about how an abuser's attention was often a survivor's first foray into romantic love or sexuality? How can we address what romantic love means to us from our abuse history in a way that doesn't result in self-judgment or others judging us? Let's not just talk about the sexuality that was affected by abuse, but the perception of what romantic love is and how to shape what we can desire as adults.

When I first started writing this chapter, I had a profound and scary dream about the lock on my bedroom door when I was a teenager. When I woke up from the dream, I was still in a state of panic, anxiety, and fear. I knew the teenage Kim had to grab my clothes from the dresser drawer and run because the lock on the door was jiggling. Someone was desperate to get into my room. I went for a run to shake off the dream.

During my run, I paused for a red light on the street corner and had an epiphany: my dad had been in love with me. Not

---

[29] Robyn E. Brickel, "Having Healthy Sex and Relationships," Psychalive, accessed July 3, 2022, https://www.psychalive.org/having-healthy-sex-and-relationships-after-sexual-abuse/.

the good kind of healthy and safe father-and-daughter love that I know exists between my kids and their dad, but the twisted, wrong love.

I remembered one night during my junior year of high school. I was living with my father and had locked my bedroom door, but I sneaked out the side door to meet my friend. We didn't do anything wrong, just drove around the deserted streets of my hometown in her convertible. I was bored to hell, like most of my teenage years when I wasn't doing drugs or drinking. Then she dropped me off at home. I will never forget the image of walking up to the house. My dad had lined up all of my stuffed animals by the front door, indicating that I had been caught. My heart sunk, and I recall my teenage self thinking it was both funny and twisted.

The memory of that incident shocked me to my core. As a teenager in abuse denial, I hadn't given it much thought, but the image of my stuffed animals lined up by the door struck me as odd. For decades, the connection alluded me, but I had a realization. When I was a young girl, I used to line up my stuffed animals on either side of my bed. They were my protectors, but no matter how strong they were in formation, they were no defense against his visits. The macabre stuffed-animal congregation outside the front door reminded me of how I used to line them up on my childhood bed. I never questioned how he found out I wasn't in my room that night, but he must have knocked, and when I didn't answer, he had gone through the hallway door into my room.

My father's message that night was, "How dare you abandon me? How dare you not want to return my love in this way." He was saying he was in love with me in a very sick and unhealthy way that a man should not be in love with his daughter. My relationship with him was like a wife. We went on outings to all kinds of places, and he and my mom never went on dates. He had sexual expressions with me that I assume he did not have with her.

I don't care if someone reads this and says, "You can't prove your father had romantic feelings for you." It doesn't matter whether it is true or not. He is dead. We will never know. But what matters is that you are willing to explore these types of dark revelations to give yourself courage to test the waters of what causes you pain and frustrates you in your adult romantic relationships. When you dig down into the crossed signals of unhealthy love during your formative years, you will instinctively know what kind of baggage and false messaging you bring to a relationship and can spot if you are attracting unhealthy people. They may be controlling, or withhold sex, or are too physical, or are emotionally shut down. Your reactions, which are often magnified, will quickly reveal what your messaging in abuse taught you. You are fighting against behaviors that indicate you should simply leave the relationship. You deserve better.

We ignore red flags because it is painful to admit we are attracted to qualities our abusers had. My dad had a hot and cold personality and would punish with silent scorn. He was depressed, and he could be sullen and hard to read. Then he would switch and be funny and smart. He would be there for me and then shut me down. It was a mixed bag. So when I dated men with erratic personalities, I thought I was being "good" as long as I served my purpose of showing up. I had no idea how to be in an equal partnership where both people asked for their needs to be met in a loving equal manner that served the love they fostered between them.

In order to aspire to a mind-blowing romantic connection, you can strive to know exactly what you want from a partner, how you want to be treated, and to not waver in your confidence. You can retrain yourself to use your voice and be aware in all of your interactions so you can learn something from everyone you date or fall in love with. The path you take to understand romantic love is a courageous one, and it is such a powerful teacher.

THE BENEFITS OF PERIODIC CELIBACY

We have a lifetime of reactions that we need to put to bed to cultivate and tap into the purest essence of ourselves that craves love and connection. We are peeling back the layers to claim who we are as our own glorious selves in perfectly aligned bodies deserving of love and sex. I am not going to let the rest of my life go by in a sad shell of what was repressed inside of me for four decades. Neither will you.

Celibacy was an unexpected gateway for making time to hold space for myself. My value was always being measured by whether or not I had a boyfriend. My warped sexual desire developed into the fundamental belief that sex is the commodity for romantic love. I had no idea that at the deepest core of my being was a beautiful, sensual woman dying to come out. For decades, I was routinely sexual, subconsciously believing that if I stopped having sex, I would be empty and alone because I had given sexual intimacy to my adult abuser during my formative years. If I wasn't giving sex, then what was I? What was my body's purpose?

I would sit in AA meetings and listen to women share their stories about drinking and having sex. When I was thirteen, I'd walk five miles down long farm roads in my hometown to my boyfriend's house to give him a blow job. I needed to expose myself to the world of men who could compliment me on my sexual skills and who were not my dad. When I was seventeen, I would scream at boyfriends who, in my perception, did not fuck or love me enough. "You don't want to give me love? You don't want to fuck me? Fuck you," I would scream on public streets, jumping out of moving cars, running off late night in foreign cities.

In young adulthood, I was very proud of my willingness to have sex in public places and keeping track of a sex count every week. Sex became part of my survival strategy to never slow down and face my demons. It was another additive to the lies. There was no grace, light, God, or love in any of it. Sex and Love Addicts Anonymous (SLAA) was a big saving grace for me in the beginning of my abuse recovery. I could shed the shame of my past while also creating the path for new ideals. I started SLAA the same year as the abuse dream (and pre-sobriety), so I hadn't dated very much. I dated two men from SLAA, and even though that wasn't the healthiest idea, we grew together until we outgrew each other. We had shared pain of our childhoods and our adulthoods, but there was too much trauma. I would lose myself in their problems, delaying this beautiful journey that I needed to take for myself. When one of them broke up with me (by email, no less), it knocked me on my ass. I talked to a few female friends and decided to hold myself accountable to them. Celibacy was suggested, and after my initial horror at the thought, I took a full year off from all men and decided to fall in love with myself. Falling in love with me was one of the hardest challenges I'd ever faced, but it was also one of the best decisions I have ever made.

During this time of celibacy, it was scary to realize how much I obsessed about a man wanting and needing me, just as the relationship with my dad had played out so many times, and also in some unsaid twisted codependence in my adult relationship with him. But everything changed when I was celibate. The constant stream of analysis and fear with male partners vanished, and I was able to see my life path clearly and connect with God, my life callings, and my sobriety in new ways. What was so cool about this period in my life—a very precious time, as lonely as it could be—was that I now had it to hold on to and give me strength. I can always make it on my own two feet. It's not that scary. Being in a romantic relationship adds value to my life, but it is not *the* value.

After a year of celibacy, I started dating again in 2015. I had never dated through an app, but I needed to learn about men as people, of all kinds and types. I had choices instead of just going with who picked me or whom I had sex with. I was faced with new, big-girl stuff—like STD tests and birth control options—that I had not really dealt with in my marriages or in my serial monogamy. It was my responsibility to take care of my body and allow a man into my full life.

Celibacy had given me the gift of perspective that men were human, just like me, who were doing the best they could to be loved. I stopped seeing men as loathsome creatures who were out to make my life miserable when they didn't do what I wanted, or didn't tell me they loved me, or constantly talked about their ex-wives. The most painful part of accepting my second divorce was realizing that my ex-husband didn't really love me deeply in a romantic sense, but how could he? I was a rageful, untreated alcoholic who kept the secret of my sexual abuse hidden. We came together to make our beautiful children and align some kind of soul contract, but it was painful to spend a decade with someone who didn't love me in the way I knew deep down in my unconscious that I deserved.

My dating experiences were a mixed bag. Some never got past phone dates, while others would ghost me after four dates. They usually bailed after any conversation about sexuality or intimacy. I wanted to know who they were before I got sexual with them. They left when they realized I wasn't going to be a fun sex girl. I was asserting my abstinence with men who I thought had potential. Still, they were far from my worthy values. I ignored big red flags, such as swearing too much, drinking too much, or clearly harboring resentments toward a cheating ex. Regardless, these men were practice ground, and I did them no harm. We often had fun until the fun was done.

There are always lessons to learn, especially if you stretch your neck out. I would go through periods of loneliness, which would grip at me, especially on the weekends when my kids would go to their dad's. It took me a long time to understand that I could be perfectly happy planning a concert with a girlfriend or going to the beach alone. It wasn't "sad" that I was alone. During the time with myself, I accepted I was a divorced mom with two children who had lots of history and stories, and I was discovering what I liked in all areas. A friend told me that I didn't need to be in charge of my love life because the serendipities had it handled. I just needed to wear lipstick and show up.

As survivors, we get to rewrite our story about romantic love, but also about the love we have for ourselves first. I encourage you to be curious in all areas of your life, including this one, but take it slow. Look at your relationship with sex and ask how it's filling you today. You can take a break and trust that you can engage in a safe way again when you are ready.

HAVING A CHOICE

I completely respect those of you in recovery from sexual abuse who have no desire for romantic relationships because of the struggle of feeling safe. Struggling is exhausting and takes the joy out of romantic love. We want to leave the struggle behind and enter into the part of romantic love that brings us the fulfillment and joy we deserve. When you are recovering from sexual abuse, what is the fine line between being "abused" or "used" in romantic love? When do you know if it feels right? We had no choices when it came to abuse when we were children. You now have choices, but will you make them as a victim or as a courageous survivor with smarts and confidence?

The key is you have the option to *stop* seeing someone if it is causing too many sleepless nights or despair. You can say in a loving way, "I'm sorry. I need a break. This is painful for me, and I would like to revisit this when I have some peace." You couldn't easily walk away from the abuse, but you can now walk away from a romantic relationship that isn't working for you if you have built the survivor power of your core self.

After dating a variety of people and having a few three-month flings, I decided it was time to only focus on men who embodied the qualities of my vision, and if I wanted sex, I could find a booty call. I didn't hold back on my list of qualities. Why should we? We are amazing people with lots of incredible assets to bring to a relationship, so why would we not eventually find a great partner to match our level of integrity?

On my list were qualities such as a sense of humor, a desire for marriage, adventurous, spiritual, makes good money and has a nice house, optimistic, kind, and admired by his peers. The list was surprisingly long, and after I finished it, I thought, *Why don't I believe this person is out there for me?* I established some personal boundaries and rules because I knew my patterns with men indicated I would self-abandon if I wanted someone to like me. I suffered whenever I broke a rule, such as don't date a man who makes you do all the planning and is too casual with your time, because I was blinded by the qualities I was attracted to and ignored the red flags. I would negotiate with myself.

It's very important to stick to your values and rules because you can suffer and experience emotional pain when you cave. Don't be too hard on yourself if this happens. If you can be introspective, you will eventually be given another chance to make a different choice, and you will look away from the wrong fit.

Think about all the qualities you are looking for in a partner. Don't hold back. If you are looking for someone who can help you financially, so be it. Why not look for someone who can engage in long, intelligent talks but also has rock hard abs? The key is to understand that while you are choosing someone based on your preferences, someone is also picking you. If the stars are lining up, you'll find someone who is your match. But the challenge is being able to ask for what you want and speak up if you have questions or confusion.

Trust in the power of manifestation, but be ready and willing to explore trust and intimacy. If someone leaves because you dug deep in a healthy way, move on. They are not ready for you.

DATING SURVIVORS

We are survivors, but that doesn't mean we can handle or want to date other survivors. We are drawn to the pain of those who have experienced trauma and abuse because we recognize it as something similar or familiar. I am not suggesting you should run away from a relationship if you find out the person you are with has been abused, but it is equally important that they are willing to heal and do the work too. If not, the person's behavior will be conflicted and confused, which could also trigger you. You need to make the choice to take care of your recovery first and leave the relationship if the person is clearly in denial of their trauma. It's also possible that the person is still in the early stages of recovery, and they are not ready to be in a relationship.

I didn't understand this until I dated a man who was facing flashbacks of abuse from his past with a female parental figure. He had not been with a romantic or sexual partner in a decade, so he had no idea these issues would surface in intimacy. But in recovery, I was able to understand the volume in which he turned up the heat with me because of his history with trauma. He engaged in the classic love bombing, telling me he loved me way too soon, and exhibiting a lack of emotional maturity. We had to end our relationship because he couldn't grow into an adult romantic relationship after the initial "teen love" phase. We felt getting better alone was his best path. I knew the long road he had ahead of him, and I prayed for his healing.

This relationship made me realize that I have been trauma bonding, or love bombing, in the past. I also realized the different ways partners can react in a relationship based on the kind of abuse they had endured.

One man I dated had intense medical issues as a child and spent lonely years in a hospital feeling neglected by his parents. Another man I dated was shut down to romantic intimacy because of his violent mother, and he would almost manically tell the same stories over and over and had a lot of ex-girlfriends hanging around. With each experience, I looked in the mirror and began to shape my own ideals.

"What would it look like to be in a relationship with me?" I would ask. After a lifetime of denial, the aftermath of past abuse no longer blows up a relationship. I still have trust issues, but that is a human condition.

In my personal experience, I discovered that in order to start a path toward long-term, healthy relationships, I had to be okay with slow and steady. I can't share everything about myself right away, and I definitely don't jump into bed so quickly. I worked hard to find a balance between being okay with the unknown progression of a relationship and having fun with my sexuality.

I am not saying that you shouldn't tell someone you are serious with or planning to marry about your abuse. Don't keep your abuse a secret. My marriages clearly suffered because of my repression of my secret. While it may not be necessary to share this information on date four or even in six months into the relationship, I strongly suggest you get this information on the table before you marry someone. If the love foundation is strong, this information will not change the love you have built. Your recovery is the foundation upon which you can freely love as an adult. Your relationship doesn't have to be diminished by trauma stories and secrets. For a while, men were attracted to me to somehow heal them from their repressed marriages. My role is not to be a healer, but I am also aware that every relationship in some way has healed me. We heal with each other and grow in a romantic partnership. It doesn't come from trauma-bonding but from honor and value. If the relationship has legs to go the distance, the secrets will be revealed gradually over time.

Lately, several of my female friends' marriages have crumbled to the ground in heartbreaking ways because their husbands haven't dealt with their own sexual abuse trauma. The pain manifests itself in mistreatment of their wives, and they become the very monsters who abused them by abandoning their families either through infidelity, verbal cruelty, psychotic breaks, and silence. If they had spoken up, they could have found partners who were willing to do whatever it took to help them get well. My friends wanted their families to stay together, but instead they were left holding the pieces of broken homes and are now coparenting little kids. I know the story well because I have been in that role.

WHAT ARE YOUR ROMANTIC RULES?

We don't want to make so many rules that we end up like birds in a gilded cage. We are already hesitant to be in love because of the trauma, or we have terrible boundaries so we get stung one time too many. Making a few romantic rules can give you a voice, and then you can evaluate how someone accepts that boundary you've set. Over time, you will eventually be able to ask for what you want and need with affirming statements like, "It feels good for me when . . ."

Write a list of your romantic rules. Some examples could be:

- I won't have sex until the fourth date.

- I like to be called or texted the next morning after a date.

- I won't date someone who stares at other people when we are out.

- I don't want to date someone with young children.

- It's unacceptable to me if the person I'm dating watches porn.

THOUGHT-PROVOKING QUESTIONS

Have you ever tried to be celibate? If you are currently not sexual or have not been for a long time, think about the relationship you have with your body right now. How do you celebrate all its inner workings, curves, and strengths?

Have you dated while you are in recovery? Even if you are married, do you go on dates with your partner? Do you go on dates with yourself?

What relationships have you stayed in for too long even when you intuitively knew your partner was treating you in questionable ways? Have you treated your partner poorly?

Do you feel compelled to trauma-bond over your abuse with your dating partner? How do you feel if you don't share your story? Do you feel like you are keeping a secret?

Chapter 20

RELEASED

A cceptance that the abuse happened may not come easy for you. Or you may find acceptance comes swiftly after doing the work on letting go of the pain of abuse. For some, acceptance can lead to forgiveness. For others, accepting that the abuse happened may never lead to forgiveness. The timeline may not be obvious. Don't put pressure on yourself to forgive and get on with it. If you are a spiritual person and believe in the exchange of energy and DNA, then you may believe that the abuser's spirit remains in you until you release it.

We don't need their energy or memory as part of our makeup. There are many different types of ways to release and forgive, or to not forgive, that feels safe and complete for you. There are energy practices for releasing pain and blocks in the body that could be preventing you from living your life to the fullest. Some of these practices I outline in this chapter may work for you, while others may not. The point is that there are many ways to connect to our inner spirit and soul to do the work that aligns us with who we are once we are free of the abuse denial.

FORGIVING AND THE UNFORGIVING

On Father's Day in 2016, ten years after my dad died of a heart attack, his energy appeared to me, and I was able to soften further into acceptance and forgiveness. It happened during an open-eye meditation. I recall the feeling that came through me as my teacher and I connected our energies in that powerful space. I felt my dad's spirit was finally healed. I felt that he was giving me the message that he now could send good and light to me. As I sat in the meditation, I thought, *Have I finally done the deep work to release myself from that abusive relationship?*

I believe my father's spirit is healing in heaven and it soothed my heart on that day. Releasing my dad's soul disentangles mine. My vision—my feeling in this meditation—was forgiveness based on my own father's spirit forgiving himself. He loathed himself, and each time he abused me, he instilled that self-loathing into me. He reached out in this meditation with an attempt to finally be a father who would guide a daughter to love herself on this earth, and to be a strong, confident woman. I heard my father's voice say, "Go learn how to be treated." In that moment, I released myself. Not everyone will be able to forgive their abuser, but this experience showed me how I could embrace forgiveness by seeing my abuser as a lost soul. I did not forgive the abusive acts, but I saw how holding on to pain took my life away from me. I could also lean into how metaphysical the experience was versus expecting myself to forgive a human in the flesh.

The following weekend, as I watched my two young daughters and their friend run down a hill by a lake while a kite floated behind them, I went through a bit of grief at how long the abuse had been a part of who I was and how I carried my body. How burdened I was by shame and regret. I was in the process that began in the meditation to mourn my damaged childhood on another level. I was grateful that my children were innocents, unburdened by the darkness of sexual abuse. They were free to think of themselves in innocence, with their imaginations, play, and exploration. They may not understand their range of emotions, but at least they have them all to themselves. I was grateful my awareness and recovery had made me vigilant in protecting them to ensure they had a childhood that was complete. As I watched my children running with the kite, I smiled. I was so happy their lives are not filled with abuse. It made me feel hope.

Later as we paddle-boated in the warm summer sun and under the spray of the lake's projectile fountain, a thought ran through my head: *A man knowing of my existence completes me.* My father's abuse had made me believe I needed a man's attention to be complete from childhood into adulthood. A wave of sadness washed over me as I yearned for an innocent childhood devoid of the abuse. The root cause of my codependency with men was the unhealthy hook on my dad that overshadowed my existence throughout childhood. These epiphanies would not have occurred if I had not been pushing through boundaries and insisting on having fun with myself, my children, or my friends. Not just in a romantic paradigm. My idea of going out, seeing the arts, exploring, and being seen just as me as a unit all to herself was entirely of my own doing. I may not have had a childhood that was clean and clear of attachment to male adult love, but I could have my own adulthood free of codependent romantic validation.

Now to truly release, I had to expand my circle. In the last four years of abuse recovery, I had closed the circle of my life pretty tight. To get sober and to heal from trauma, I had to create a safe container to release so much pain and emotion. One week after that meditative connection with my dad, I had two epiphanies. The first was that I wanted to start traveling internationally again (I had not traveled since sobriety). The second was the realization that just because I had tapped into some forgiveness in that meditation, I didn't have to forgive my dad completely. I could have a range of emotions and be okay. I had gone through the process of justifying his own possible abuse history (perhaps he had been abused himself), but I wasn't truly owning the forgiveness. Yet, this could no longer hold me back from living a full life. I had to move on even in the unforgiving.

I thought, *Wow, life is going to get big for me again. Can I walk into the world knowing there is good and there is bad?* All my previous adventures were not for naught. They shaped me into the full visionary I am today to hold space for people's visions. My concern now wasn't having fun; it was opening my net and my world to meet people for all sorts of reasons. I saw that the lines could blur, but all the parts had to be there. To get to the other side of release, I had to totally surrender to all of my feelings about my dad and own them.

"My father did me a favor by dying," I said to a friend one day.

He paused. "I'm speechless," he said. "And that is rare."

"I'm sorry," I said, "But it is the truth, and not in a cruel way."

"I can hear that," he said. "In the way you spoke."

It was true, and I had to put in the work to not go into a shame and fear spiral about the truth of that statement. I felt pulled to sympathize and hedge, but that was part of my denial. I could love my dad for the parts of him I had once cherished as a child, but I could also be happy he was dead. He was my abuser. If he were alive today, I may not have come to terms with the abuse. Our suffering together on this earth was too great. Someone had to go, and it was not me. I was grateful God stepped in and did his work to remove my dad in his physical body. Yet, I was still energetically holding myself back from an incredible life. I saw it was time to step out in a bigger way.

ENERGY PRACTICES

I have released in many degrees since I faced my sexual abuse. I have found joy in some of the strangest, unexpected commitments and created circles of trust in unlikely places. I have released the shame of divorce and am able to coparent effectively with my ex-husband every week to ensure our daughters have healthy and prosperous childhoods into adulthood. I have released any beliefs that my life is small or confined, and if I can dream it, I can have it. When we were trapped in the dark closet of our sexual abuse, all we could really see was a life where we didn't feel so hopeless and sad. That is your base. Once you access the light, you'll start releasing all that doesn't serve you and can then focus in on what you want. The world is here for you now. Grab it!

I engaged in a bunch of practices to help move the energy through my body that may have lingered after I had faced the abuse. I had to release residual energy and be in a place where I could grieve and mourn to my fullest capacity. In some cases, that had to look raw and without an agenda.

Here are a few of the practices I engaged in over the course of recovery that continued to aid in my energy release. Remember, as you step out into a bigger life and pursue more of what you deserve in romance, finance, religion, friendships, and inner peace, a lifetime of stored energy will need to be addressed and released.

Breathwork

I went to a women's AA retreat where there was a profound breathing workshop for trauma. We were all sitting on our yoga mats on the floor. The facilitator asked us to set an intention, and I set mine to no longer have my father be a part of my DNA.

I said to him, "I know you are dead, but now it is time to really put you to rest."

I made the assertion that my dad could no longer have power over me—a power that evoked a lifetime of rage at my primary male role model's failure to treat me with kindness, safety, and reverence that a father should. When I was a little girl, his foul moods were scary. Then he was affectionate. He had been my lover in a sick, dark place. I wouldn't have it anymore. No longer did my inner child have to cope with a daddy who loved her one minute and was cruel and mean the next. There was no light in the darkest of those shadows. It just had to be brightened. I wouldn't live in the cold dampness anymore. I was born with his spunk, charisma, sexuality, and intelligence, but I would no longer apply the patterns to the romantic experiences I craved.

I started crying when the practitioner turned on the music. She said this would happen. The deep belly-chest-mouth breath causes your hands to lose feeling and your brain to be numb, and you just feel this deep release and sadness. I know that I got rid of a lot of him in that session. My chest got damp and my vagina was wet (yet not wet, just the sensation in my pants). I walked away from the breathing exercise exhausted, but I knew I was sane, whole, and complete. I didn't feel my dad's hold on me. Only a few months later would he be fully released through the open-eye meditation.

Past-Life Regressions

There are many legitimate and respected practices that can help heal body trauma, such as acupuncture or craniosacral therapy. I was guided to less obvious routes of healing and made the decision to not question my instincts around healing. I felt like I needed to release different identities from past lifetimes in order to have a clear channel of communication with my newly claimed body and identity. I used to not believe in any of this stuff, but throughout my recovery, I felt drawn to the idea that I was carrying some heavy burden that felt not of this world. Abuse survivors are more vulnerable to other people's energy attaching to us because of the disassociation in the abuse and the fracturing of our psyche. I would even venture to say that many of us are empaths. All I ask is that you keep an open mind when reading about my past-life regressions.

I entrusted in my friend Gale to do some energy and spiritual work. First, Gale removed some hooks that people had energetically placed in me, and also a few curses. It became apparent that being released played into my recovery.

When we did the regression, I told Gale what I saw from my past lives. I can't explain how trippy it was to suddenly talk about being a witch and living in this dark space with my children dying of dysentery, and that I was going to be burned at the stake and how hopeless it all was. In the vision, I saw myself writing furiously, leaving evidence of my innocence as I tried to write down the history. I was sad for this Kim the witch. We then erased that past by creating a new one where I was a successful, happily married songwriter in London, and I owned a blue Rolls-Royce from money earned through my career. I walked away with a more energetic, whole feeling about the me who had lived more lifetimes than this one. I understood how precious each lifetime is and wanted to make the most of it by not allowing the abuse energy to hold me back.

Harmonyum

This modality was divinely offered to me with just a little bit of seeking. I was trying out a new yoga studio in Santa Monica after my longtime teacher closed up shop. I met a Harmonyum practitioner when she signed me up for a yoga class. I decided to try a few sessions based on how I felt energetically around her. I had an instinct she belonged on my recovery path.

Harmonyum is a practice of deep energy work that sends healing to the nervous system and the brain. You enter a dark room and lie down on a table. All you have to do is lie there for an hour while the practitioner runs her hands around your body

energy without touching you. You can feel profound shifts—
some soothing, some uncomfortable. When I did energy work
early in my recovery, I was attempting to release energy that I
had stored up since childhood. In the Harmonyum sessions, I was
releasing lighter waves of energy that allowed me to continue
growing and expanding into the confident, happy woman I had
started to become.

Even if Harmonyum healing is not your cup of tea, energy
work can be a powerful, beautiful thing because you get to trust
another human being with your body who has your best interests
at heart. It's not a massage, which for some can be triggering, but
rather a beautiful energy exchange.

MONEY BLOCKS

In order to take care of your whole soul, abuse needs to be
released from every single area of your life because they were
all touched. It's time to release the state of denial you have been
in for so long. Then you can move into every nook and cranny
of your heart and soul until there are no longer any remnants of
the abuse.

One of the major roadblocks is limited earning power and
erratic financial decisions. Part of learning who you can be
financially in the world is releasing the burdens or the knowledge about finances that have been engrained in us from our
childhood conditioning. The abuse has told us we are not rock-
star, high-income-producing leaders. I had struggled with not
earning enough money as a young adult. Until I faced the abuse
denial, I made excuses. No one helped me with finances, the
film business paid so little, and I grew up imprinted by my dad's
crappy, impulsive business decisions (he died owing the IRS tens
of thousands of dollars). I took on the identity of an under-earner
and expected I would experience financial tragedy.

Releasing my dad as my abuser freed me from my tie to parental money struggles. I was not him. I was not my mother. I could create a happy, lucrative home environment. I could create my own money mantras and visions for my future. I could remain modestly successful financially as an abuse survivor, or I could become a first-generation millionaire. The choice was up to me and how hard I wanted to work.

Releasing my dad's hold on me allowed me to see that I could break the pattern of financial insecurity. I started to invest money directly into my own personal development. I looked at how I could save or invest money in a different way than when I was in abuse denial. I got curious about what it would take to buy a house or go on an international vacation. You may want to put some money aside so you can take a spa day once a month.

I took a course on money management and saw holes where I thought I had control over money, but then I would fearfully overspend or go into scarcity. It was the same emotional pendulum that would swing in all areas of my life as a result from the abuse. Screwed or abandoned.

Financial fear can be released in order to fully explore all of your survivor power and pursue the life that you want to live. We need money to provide for our families, build businesses, give to charities, and see the world. Loathsome body images and depravity of life's beautiful, special little gifts must be released. Screaming at people has to be released. Berating yourself for not being enough, knowing enough, and doing enough has to be released.

INVESTING IN YOURSELF

Taking financial responsibility and releasing old energetic blocks in recovery is cultivated through tangible action toward abundant financial energy. When I was in early recovery and just starting my business, I hired a financial planner to help me understand the various financial buckets I could fill if I made a certain income. I knew I needed to figure out how to build a financial legacy way before I made any real money to play with. Those five-year projections motivated me to earn the money I needed to fill those investment buckets and plan for my retirement, as well as have some emergency funds to protect myself and my kids. I will never forget the day when I realized over the last eight years I had invested and saved over $150,000!

Here are a few steps you can take to dissolve those money blocks:

- Add a financial professional to your money team. This could be a financial planner who simply helps you plan and eventually can help you decide on investment products.

- Speak with someone in your world who appears to make sound financial choices. Invite them to coffee and ask for advice on how to stay accountable to long-term financial goals.

- Make a list of all the trips, adventures, and classes you want to take. Motivate yourself by putting a little money aside from each paycheck toward one of these goals.

You deserve to live a live free of the things that have held you captive under the guise of abuse denial. Acknowledging the energy is a good place to start. But learning how to release and let go is a new practice that gives you a new identity for a new life!

THOUGHT-PROVOKING QUESTIONS

Have you avoided holistic practices or classes that could help release you a bit more? Where have you not given yourself permission to explore?

What do you say about your abuser that is perfectly candid? What has it opened up or shut down for you?

What is your current relationship with money? Did your abuser buy you gifts, alcohol, or pay your way? Or was it the opposite, and you were neglected and deprived?

How do you invest in yourself and your happiness today?

Chapter 21
A NEW LIFE BEGINS

I told myself one big, long, cruel lie for forty-two years. I lied by omission while the abuse was happening, and I lied after it in denial. I buried the lie as deeply as one can in the recesses of my mind. The lie may have killed me, and if I hadn't discovered my spirituality, gotten sober, and strengthened my relationship with God, I wouldn't have had a shot at a real, true, honest, and full life. We have the ability to be tremendous liars in order to protect ourselves and avoid being vulnerable, but we need to be honest. It's not a protection at all to lie. It's a constant rejection of our honest selves.

At one point in my recovery, I thought I was taking my life back, but the truth was that I was no longer lying to myself. I wasn't fantasizing about some false life that was less than what I deserved. I wasn't avoiding true self-love to protect myself. I wasn't lying about the newfound ability to create the life I wanted to fully live. I was in charge. I had all the power. I did not need to give it away. Part of that work involved not only changing my old thinking, but also being honest about how happy I wanted to be. I chose to find an existence that was filled with a mindset of peace and prosperity. I stopped fighting the fight. I experienced life in an affirming, abundant, and giving way.

I still have the desire to want to protect myself. It is not a horrible trait. We can be warriors and savvy people out there in the world. It can be difficult to protect yourself against others who are safe and want to love you. You need to trust those who are good at heart and want to support you. When I don't have enough space, I tend to create false stories in my head about my reality. Sometimes it's just my alcoholism trying to isolate me, and since I don't drink or use drugs anymore, I will escape by obsessing over a guy, my finances, or a situation with my kids. Whatever your method of escape is, you don't have to hide and be alone anymore with your abuse. I hear you. We all hear you. You are no longer alone. We can become part of a community as we heal. Even when we are by ourselves, we will not feel that same sense of isolation because we are choosing to be in solitary peace. Whatever personality you have out in the world, remember that your desires and dreams make you unique. You don't have to fit into a mold or be perfect in recovery. You get to just begin again.

MY SOUL'S IDENTITY

I explored my long-buried original soul nine years into my recovery when I felt emotionally stable and attempted to surrender to being vulnerable. My journey into my true soul's identity allowed me to go deeper into the complexities of facing abuse. You do not have to wait nine years. That was how long it took me to discover this work. You will continue to face abuse in different ways, at different times, through a variety of modalities.

From my exploration of Shamanism, I learned that we are born with a soul identity. The Shamans believe we are born as a pure version of ourselves before other people's influence, expectations, judgments, and opinions affect who we are. We soon start to drift away from who we were in our original form by creating behaviors that help us navigate and survive a false sense of self. Our pure essence can be redirected by the actions of our family of origin, but also close caregivers, teachers, and religious figures.

My original soul identity was destroyed because of the abuse and the breach of trust I experienced as a child. I developed behaviors, such as uncontrolled rage and jealousy, to maintain this false identity. Throughout the years, I have done many things that are physically harmful, such as crashing vehicles, smashing technological devices, yelling at family members, having long bouts of sobbing or hangovers, and squashing any part of my voice that had a shot at leadership. I moved mountains and then I blew them up. When you believe you are dirty and unworthy of anything on this planet, you compensate by becoming drawn to the external noise that confirms your unworthiness.

I also operated without knowing my true soul because I had no inner source to tap in to other than a radical case of self-will. I would zero in on what I wanted and just make it happen. I didn't know myself well enough to put my trust in a sense of peace if I wanted to go in a certain direction in my life. My choices were fueled by a lot of black-and-white thinking. I needed to create volatile, untrusting, and unstable environments because I was moving forward but with a restlessness I couldn't identify.

Learning that I had a soul identity that could be rediscovered after being buried by the opinions, dynamics, and actions of the adult caretakers in my life was beyond liberating and gave me hope for a new beginning.

CATCHING GLIMPSES OF YOUR SOUL

The goal of this exercise is to identify times when your ego or your soul has taken center stage. Is your ego in control, or is it sitting in the passenger's seat while your soul drives? We can make healthier and happier decisions if we are aware of how we are influenced.

Here are a few things to consider when making decisions that are more soul-centered:

- Examine a behavior that you are not proud of. Maybe you

are "quick to anger" or "impatient." How would it feel to wait twenty-four hours before you react or make a decision?

- How do you respond when you consider another person's opposing viewpoint? Does your disappointment discredit your needs? Consider how you can honor both opinions.

- When you are about to engage in a negative behavior in response to a decision, stop and do the exact opposite. Put your faith in that outcome. For example, if you are prone to being angry, find compassion. If you are rushing someone out of impatience, slow down.

When you oppose these impulsive behaviors, you put yourself in a more receptive position to be aware of what you see, hear, and do. You will reveal to yourself more of your true soul's essence in these kinder and gentler spaces.

The key in my life when I show up for my business, my kids, my life partner, and my friends is to be fully 100 percent present and to be okay with all the feelings in my mind and body that come along for the ride. I can be with others because they are not going to abuse me. Even if you talk to me in a way I don't like or have an opinion I disagree with, you are not my dad forcing me to lie there while you defile me. We need to trust people again and join the energies of love in the world so we can project the power of who we are as survivors into the global space.

You are not a bad person. I am not a bad person. I was never a bad girl because I was abused. I deserve all the same benefits and considerations as every other human on this planet. I am no longer a half human. I don't carry any more secrets. I live a very sane and honorable life. You can too. You will, and it will all be okay.

I pray for enough healing in all of us survivors so we can have empathy and compassion for the men and women who are still trapped inside their old story, who believe they can't have any love other than that primal initial love of their sexual abuser. It is so hard to break that old story. Our journey can help them by example. We can kick abuse in the ass.

Today, as I continue to recover from sexual abuse denial, I have an intuition and a gut feeling that aligns with the me I have discovered in this process. I have an adult mind and a body that is connected. In the past, I was completely disconnected from physical and mental cues and didn't trust any I received. My mind and body did not talk to each other.

Today, I apply that intuitive feeling to evaluate people and their motivations. When I find myself in situations with people who are erratic, addictive, and abusive, it only takes me three weeks to walk away versus forty years. I am sharply attuned to my inner self, so I seek out companions who nourish me, and my expectations of others come from a place of connection rather than how I can use them to feel better or to hide myself. I no longer want to operate with a dark secret agenda. I want to walk in the transparency of my soul so I can be a vessel for survivors who are still seeking their path.

Walk in the deepest wild of yourself. Make choices to cultivate the most profound life. Waste no more time, dear heart, for today, in this very moment, your body is your own.

We are all survivors of some form of abuse. Today, we get to have voices and speak out. With that right, we can have love and live freely where limits have no bounds. I love you, wherever you are, and together we can find gratitude in this journey.

BIBLIOGRAPHY

Alcoholics Anonymous: The Big Book. Alcoholics Anonymous World Services, Inc., 2002.

Brickel, Robyn E. "Having Healthy Sex and Relationships." Psychalive. Accessed July 3, 2022. https://www.psychalive.org/having-healthy-sex-and-relationships-after-sexual-abuse/.

Brooks, Rachel. *Chasing Perfection: A Journey to Healing, Fitness, and Self-Love*. Ohio: Author Academy Elite, 2020.

Browne, Sarah Jeanne. "5 Self-Soothing Tips to Heal Your Inner Child." *Forbes*, September 2, 2021. https://www.forbes.com/sites/womensmedia/2021/09/02/5-self-soothing-tips-to-heal-your-inner-child/.

Casey, Shaun. "12 Ways to Make Time for Listening Partnerships (And Make Parenting Easier)," Hand in Hand Parenting. November 21, 2021. https://www.handinhandparenting.org/2021/11/12-ways-to-make-time-for-listening-partnerships-and-make-parenting-easier/.

Centers for Disease Control and Prevention. "Genital Herpes." CDC Detailed Fact Sheet. Accessed August 21, 2022. https://www.cdc.gov/std/herpes/stdfact-herpes-detailed.htm#ref1.

HAVOCA. "Telling Our Family, Friends, and Acquaintances About Our Abuse." Accessed August 21, 2022. https://www.havoca.org/first-step/telling-others/.

Hay, Louise. *You Can Heal Your Life*. Hay House Publishing, 2008.

International Society for Traumatic Stress Studies. "Recovered Memories of Childhood Trauma." Accessed July 1, 2022, https://istss.org/public-resources/trauma-basics/what-is-childhood-trauma/remembering-childhood-trauma.

Johnson, Brianna. "Are You a Chronic Self-Abandoner?" April 30, 2018. https://www.nami.org/Blogs/NAMI-Blog/April-2018/Are-You-a-Chronic-Self-Abandoner.

Joseph, Naomi. *Binge and Sprint: From Endless Cake to Recovery*. WriteLife Publishing, 2021.

Khazan, Olga. "The Second Assault." *The Atlantic,* December 15, 2015. https://www.theatlantic.com/health/archive/2015/12/sexual-abuse-victims-obesity/420186/.

Meloy, Satre Rena. "Balancing Our Feminine and Masculine Energy." Pause. Accessed July 1, 2022. https://www.pausemeditation.org/single-post/balancing-feminine-masculine-energy.

Raising Children. "Child development: the first five years." Accessed, July 2, 2022. https://raisingchildren.net.au/newborns/development/understanding-development/development-first-five-years.

Rubin, Bruce Joel. YouTube. https://www.youtube.com/c/BruceJoelRubin/videos.

Saprea. "The Effects of Child Sexual Abuse: Shame and Child Sexual Abuse." Accessed August 21, 2022. https://youniquefoundation.org/resources-for-child-sexual-abuse-survivors/effects-of-child-sexual-abuse/shame-and-child-sexual-abuse/.

Singer, Michael A. *The Surrender Experiment: My Journey into Life's Perfection.* New York: Harmony Books, 2015.

Stanford Graduate School of Business. "Oprah Winfrey on Career, Life, and Leadership." April 28, 2014. YouTube video. https://www.youtube.com/watch?v=6DlrqeWrczs.

Stiles, Cara L. "The Influence of Childhood Dissociative States from Sexual Abuse on the Adult Woman's Spiritual Development." *Journal of Heart Centered Therapies* 10, no. 1 (2007). https://go.gale.com/ps/i.

Stone, Emma. "The Emerging Science of Awe and Its Benefits." *Psychology Today,* April 27, 2017. https://www.psychologytoday.com/us/blog/understanding-awe/201704/the-emerging-science-awe-and-its-benefits.

Survivors Voices. "Responses." Accessed November 4, 2022. https://survivorsvoices.ca/responses/.

Twenty-Four Hours a Day. Center City: Hazelden Publishing, 2019.

Zukav, Gary. *The Seat of the Soul: An Inspiring Vision of Humanity's Spiritual Destiny.* Rider Classics, 2022. Kindle.

RECOMMENDED READING

Butterworth, Eric. *Discover the Power Within You: A Guide to the Unexplored Depths Within.* Harper Collins, 2010. Kindle.

ACKNOWLEDGMENTS

I would first like to extend my deepest love to my two daughters who inspire me every day with their wisdom. We have traveled, belly laughed until our stomachs ached, and have grown together in this process. I am eternally grateful that we are a new legacy of joy and trust in our unit today. I get to show them how a woman who comes from trauma and addiction can create a big, wonderful life.

The strength required to finish this book came in stages. Stephanie Zhong and Nancy Manpearl showed me love, kindness, and support in the early drafts. They were quick to remind me to love myself when my old thinking, denial, and limiting beliefs were in charge. When I was considering releasing this book, the perseverance and tenacity of all my book clients gave me courage to move forward. They showed me, through their books, that it is possible to write about "hard things." In the later drafts, I am grateful to the merry band of writers at Kathy Katims's Saved By A Story workshops for listening to me share my chapters and cheering me on. Allison Itterly, my editor at WriteLife Publishing, was my rock. She was smart, insightful, kind, and firm. She would also field emails from me about times when my heart felt like it was breaking and put me back on track with her kind words.

I am forever grateful to God for showing me daily miracles. He has guided me to the right path to many healers, including the shamanic practices of Steve Bull and Sally Denny. The soul-retrieval work I did with them changed my life and set this book on its final course. I was also divinely led while writing the last drafts of this book to Sister Michelle Long at the Hope in Christ Community Church in Compton, California, where I now routinely go to sing, pray, and heal. I unexpectedly found a spiritual home through the ministry of Pastor Isaiah Robertson and the Sunday School led by Sister Sharon Lewis.

I am forever grateful to my trauma therapist, Rena K. When she agreed to work with me shortly after I faced the abuse, she took on a lifetime of denial, sadness, and anger. I can't express enough how much she taught me what it was like to be truly loved without any judgment, and then set me free to start living. I also thank fellow author Naomi Joseph for taking my calls and voice memos when I felt afraid about how I was changing in recovery and assuring me I was God's child. I mention AA a lot in the book, and I would be nowhere without Twelve Steps, so thank you Bill W. for writing *The Big Book*.

ABOUT THE AUTHOR

Kim O'Hara, Book Coach to Best Sellers™, has been a storyteller for over thirty years with a previous two-decades-long career as a film producer and screenwriter. Today, she guides her clients through writing best-selling books. Her authors have been on the *Wall Street Journal* top ten business books lists, *USA Today* top 150, and numerous Amazon #1 bestseller lists in nonfiction. She hosts a successful podcast, *You Should Write a Book About That*™, interviewing fascinating people with a story to tell. She lives with her two daughters in South Los Angeles in a house she proudly bought as a single woman. She is currently writing a book about her house-buying journey.